THE
EMERGING
ROLE
OF
DEACONS

Charles W. Deweese

BROADMAN
& HOLMAN
PUBLISHERS

Nashville, Tennessee

Dewey Decimal Classification: 262.1

Subject heading: DEACONS

To
Murray Clinton Eisenhauer
father-in-law
and
deacon
First Baptist Church
Asheville, North Carolina

Contents

Preface

The New Testament provides a clear reason for the appearance of deacons. They are special church servants. The high qualifications expected of them suggest that they are also to be leaders in congregational life. While the primary purposes of this book are to portray deacon trends of the past and present and to offer some practical possibilities for future deacon development, the beginning point is the Bible. Here lies the standard by which all deacon life must be evaluated.

The emerging role of deacons has been a vital feature of Christianity since the New Testament era. Baptists have had deacons since their first churches arose in the early 1600s. As a rule, Baptist churches have tended to be only as strong as their deacon bodies. The future maturity of these churches will depend heavily on the willingness of their deacons to heed biblical qualifications, to engage in a variety of ministries, to provide high-grade leadership, and to establish an exemplary life-style.

Deacons who read this small volume will see how their colleagues in deaconship have fared through the years. They will find a positive affirmation of the biblical values of their office. They will discover that deacons have functioned at their best when serving tables— the table of the Lord, the table of the needy, and the table of the minister.

Several persons deserve special thanks. Initial encouragement for the writing came from Francis A. Martin, former editor of *The Deacon*. While I was on a study leave in the fall of 1978, Morse and Rita Eisenhauer graciously provided me a quiet room in their home in Lunenburg, Nova Scotia, Canada, where most of the first draft was written. The Historical Commission of the Southern Baptist Convention generously made the study leave available after I completed my first five years on the staff. E. Glenn Hinson and Leon McBeth, professors of church history at Southern Baptist Theological Seminary and Southwestern Baptist Theological Seminary, respectively, read parts of the manuscript and gave helpful guidance. Henry Webb, present editor of *The Deacon*, offered superior assistance and many hours in evaluating two editions of the complete manuscript. Most important, Mary Jane and Dana, my wife and daughter, created a supportive climate for this ministry. Julie, our other daughter, was born in the middle of chapter 3 and added spice to the remainder of the project.

Permission is gratefully acknowledged for the use of certain material from a series of articles by Charles W. Deweese which were first published in *The Deacon*, January-March 1975, through July-September 1976 (© Copyright 1974, 1975, 1976, The Sunday School Board of the Southern Baptist Convention).

Permission is also gratefully acknowledged for the use of certain material from an article by Charles W. Deweese which was first published as "Deaconesses in Baptist History: A Preliminary Study" in *Baptist History and Heritage*, January 1977 (© Copyright 1977, Historical Commission of the Southern Baptist Convention).

Unless otherwise indicated, all biblical quotations in this volume are from the Revised Standard Version.

CHARLES W. DEWEESE

1

THE BIRTH AND RISE OF DEACONS

Deacons arose in the early New Testament church to meet the need for special church servants. The Greek word translated deacon is *diakonos*, whose more general meaning is "servant." The words *dia* (through) and *konis* (dust) form the basis of *diakonos*. Perhaps the original meaning of *diakonos* was a table waiter who walked barefoot through dust to serve dining guests.

Jesus' own life serves as the model for the deacon, for he claimed that he "came not to be served but to serve" (Mark 10:45). Thus, he defined his own work as that of deaconing. Jesus went so far as to make servanthood the true sign of greatness: "Whoever would be great among you must be your servant" (Mark 10:43). *Diakonos* or one of its forms appears in both these verses dealing with the servant concept of Jesus.

Several key points emerge from the New Testament evidence concerning deacons. Although Bible scholars disagree over whether Acts 6:1-6 actually refers to deacons, virtually all agree that 1 Timothy 3:8-13 is a direct reference to them. The qualifications required of deacons were high. Deacons were closely related to bishops, or overseers, and probably were in an assistant capacity. There is no full description of the precise duties of deacons. Possible biblical references to women deacons (Rom. 16:1; 1 Tim. 3:11) are few and brief and subject to diverse interpretation.

Last, and perhaps most important, deacons belonged to the very nature and being of the church. Christ used *diakonos* to describe the ideal Christian servant (Mark 10:43). Paul spoke of apostles, prophets, evangelists, pastors, and teachers as functioning "for the equipment of the saints, for the work of *diakonia*"—or "ministry" (Eph. 4:12). The servant role to be shared broadly by church members was vital to the rise of the diaconate.

The New Testament "affords unambiguous evidence of the perpetual necessity of *diakonia* as a function of the Church on earth." [1] The New Testament church organized the work of *diakonia* in a concentrated form in the office of deacon. Deacons were not incidental to the church but were an integral part of it. The deaconing function is the basis of all ministry in the church. Deacons will continue to be essential to the church as long as Christian service is at its heart.

Since New Testament information about the ordination, role, and duties of deacons is so slim, the evidence of later Christian literature assumes an importance that cannot be underestimated. This literature reveals how individuals and churches both interpreted and implemented New Testament teachings about deacons. A close look at deacon developments in the early centuries, reasons for the decline of deacons leading to and lasting through the Middle Ages, and the recovery of the biblical significance of deacons in the Reformation period can provide many clues for enriching the ministries of contemporary deacons.

The Early Church

Material about deacons in sources from the second through the fifth centuries is especially valuable. These sources show that early deacons had duties relating to charity, administration, education, and worship. To begin with, deacons did pastoral work through being the real agents of charity for the church. They visited martyrs who were in prison, clothed and buried the dead, looked after the excommunicated with the hope of restoring them, provided for the needs of widows and orphans, and visited the sick and those who were otherwise in distress. In a plague that struck Alexandria about A.D. 259, deacons were described by an eyewitness as those who "visited the sick fearlessly," "ministered to them continually," and "died with them most joyfully." [2]

The deacon performed an extremely important duty in notifying both the bishop and the multitudes of those who were sick. In this way the deacon facilitated a more thorough ministry to the ill. A third-century deacon family ministry plan stated that "in proportion to the number of the congregation . . . , so let the deacons be" so that proper ministry could be given to all. [3]

Deacons exposed themselves to great danger in times of persecution. An ancient document describes the reaction of the deacon Habib to the order of Emperor Licinius that everyone should worship the pagan god Zeus. Habib secretly visited churches in several villages where he "ministered and read the Scriptures, and encouraged and strengthened many by his words, and admonished them to stand fast in the truth of their belief, and not to be afraid of the persecutors; and gave them directions." [4] Habib was martyred for his actions.

Further, deacons carried out administrative assignments given them by bishops. They assembled daily to receive instructions from the bishop for the day's business. They kept order in the church service, cared for the altar and its utensils, delivered messages for bishops, and administered the church fund as the executive agents of the bishop. [5]

Deacons kept a close watch on church members and reported to the bishop any member about to sin so that the bishop could approach this person and hopefully prevent the sin. In this way deacons exercised pastoral care and preventive church discipline through their administrative role. [6]

Fabian, bishop of Rome (A.D. 236-250), aided diaconal administration and ministry by dividing the city into seven districts and assigning each district to one of the seven deacons in the Roman church. He also appointed seven subdeacons to be the deacons' assistants and eventually to succeed them. This provided unbroken continuity in administration. (Subdeacons arose in large cities in the West by A.D. 200 and in the East by 350, both because deacons needed more help and because many churches interpreted Acts 6 as limiting the number of regular deacons in one place to seven.) [7]

Deacons were teachers, too. Not only did they have occasional preaching duties, but they also assisted bishops in training new converts. Augustine sent encouragement and instruction to Deogratias, a deacon in Carthage who taught new Christians.[8] One reason for the involvement of deacons in teaching converts was the heavy influx of people into the church after the time of Constantine, the first Christian emperor of the Roman Empire (A.D. 306-337).

Last, deacons had important worship responsibilities. Many early writings conceded to deacons the right to perform baptisms. A deacon could baptize under only two conditions. He had to have the authority of the bishop, and a bishop or presbyter had to be present. Normally, deacons did not baptize, since this function belonged properly to the presbyters. (The presbyter, based on the New Testament word *presbuteros*, commonly translated "elder," evolved in the early centures in the Catholic tradition into a priest who belonged to an order of ministry ranked in authority below bishops but above deacons.) [9]

Deaccns also assisted in the Lord's Supper. In the second century deacons distributed the bread and wine and carried some away to the Christians who were absent. In order that all participants might examine themselves before receiving the Supper, third-century deacons asked the congregation, "Is there any man that keepeth aught against his fellow?" This statement was the first recorded in Christian literature to be made by deacons in church. In communion the deacon prayed publicly, read the Gospels, called for the praying of the Lord's Prayer, and concluded the service by inviting the people to go forth in peace.[10]

The earliest detailed data on the ordination of deacons appeared in a third-century writing. Only a bishop, this document stated, could lay on hands at a deacon's ordination, since "he is not ordained for a priesthood, but for the service of the bishop." [11]

Deacons were expected to live pure and blameless lives before God and to be imitators of Christ by laying down their lives for their brothers in ministry. As examples of the holy life, deacons were afforded much respect. A second-century writer called for the people to honor their deacons, since the deacons were both the "appointment of Jesus Christ" and the "institution of God." In like manner, deacons were severely disciplined when they abandoned the holy life or were disobedient to bishops. For example, deacons were to be deposed if they refused to exercise any part of their assigned ministry. [12]

Women also assumed diaconal positions in the early centuries, although the exact origin of deaconesses is unknown. A third-century eastern writing was the first piece of Christian literature to describe the duties of deaconesses in detail. They were to minister primarily to women, while deacons ministered to men. They were to assist at the baptism of women, to teach newly baptized women how to live holy and pure lives, to visit sick women, and to bathe those women recovering from sickness. [13]

Deaconesses arose first in eastern countries because the seclusion of women in these areas made necessary a special ministry to them. They did not appear in the West until the fifth century and were not accepted in Rome before the eighth. The number of deaconesses grew with the increase of congregations. They were apparently drawn from the order of widows who had already developed an active ministry to female members of congregations (see 1 Tim. 5:3-16 for a New Testament discussion of widows). Deaconesses had a less important role in worship than their male counterparts and could not look forward to a higher office, as could deacons. [14]

Deaconesses were evidently not ordained in the first three centuries. Such ordination, whenever it began, was an eastern custom, for churches in the West did not ordain women. A fourth-century eastern writing presented a suggested procedure for ordaining a deaconess. After she passed a careful preliminary examination, the bishop was to lay hands upon her in the presence of the presbyters, deacons, and other deaconesses. The bishop then ended the service with an ordination prayer.[15]

The Middle Ages

Compared to the important servant functions of deacons in the early church, the role of deacons suffered a major decline in the Middle Ages (A.D. 500-1500). Several factors accounted for this decline, which actually began during the fourth and fifth centuries. An initial look at deacon developments in these two centuries is necessary, since these trends virtually determined the pattern of the medieval diaconate.

A key reason for the decline in the Eastern Church was an increased emphasis on the liturgical (worship) tasks of deacons. This stress lessened the primary role of deacons as agents of charity and practical ministries. Another cause of decline in the East was the expansion in the number of deacons. As congregations grew larger and more numerous, more deacons were required to meet the liturgical demands. Whereas deacons had held a high position when only seven were connected to a bishop, they gradually lost this status as their numbers grew and as they were scattered all over the diocese to become assistants to presbyters.[16]

The basic reason for the decline of deacons in the Western Church was the rise of the view of the ministry as a *cursus honorum* (course of honors), which took place in the fourth century. This idea probably imitated the political *cursus honorum* of the Roman civil servants in the Christianized state set up by Emperor Constantine. The *cursus honorum* implied a succession of steps, each of which had to be reached before attaining the one above it. The diaconate "could no longer be considered a terminal or life ministry. It was merely a rung in the clerical ladder." [17] An early prayer for the ordination of deacons included a petition that they might become worthy to merit promotion to a higher rank.[18]

In the context of this bureaucracy, the diaconate suffered a change which had negative results for hundreds of years. Instead of remaining an important approach to Christian service in its own right, the diaconate simply became the first stage in the move toward the priesthood. Although the church orders (deacons, presbyters, bishops) were previously regarded as functions instead of offices, with no one order having more spiritual significance than another, growth in the church led to grades of ministry and to the subordination of function to office, position, and privilege.[19]

The introduction of the principle of "hierarchy" finally placed the deacon below the presbyter as an inferior minister. It also destroyed the principle of "organism" in which the ministry of each congregation was viewed as an organic whole whose parts were not interchangeable but had essential and distinctive functions. Further, it opened for deacons the possibility of a career in the clergy and raised a professional distinction between clergy and laity.[20]

Another factor also led to the decline of deacons in the West. While the multiplication of deacons in the East worked to their detriment, the restricting of deacons to just seven in such places as Rome created a contrasting problem. Since the presbyters in Rome had become the principal recipients of episcopal powers and the seven deacons there had little power, these deacons resorted to abuses of their position and tried many times in the fourth century to make themselves superior to the more numerous and highly paid presbyters.[21]

Councils composed of representatives from churches in various areas then began to restrict further the role and status of deacons. To illustrate, after finding that some deacons in Rome and other places were administering the Lord's Supper to presbyters, the Council of Nicaea (A.D. 325) both disallowed this and asserted further that deacons should not even sit among the presbyters, since they were inferior to them.[22]

Several factors also led to the decline of deaconesses in the East and West. Because of the close relationship between deacons and deaconesses, the decline of the former had inevitable consequences for the latter. The rise of an ecclesiastical hierarchy in the West worked against deaconesses there, since women could not be ordained to the priesthood. Since one of their most important functions was to assist in the baptism of women, deaconesses became less significant as believer's baptism by immersion gave way to the rise of infant baptism. Last, the growth of cloistered communities provided places of withdrawal for devout women who felt a distinct religious calling.[23]

After the fourth and fifth centuries and on into the Middle Ages, the influence of deacons diminished severely, and their chief role became more and more liturgical. One factor in this continuing shift in function was the rise of monastic orders which assumed many of the caring and practical ministries formerly carried out by deacons. A *diakonia* (ministry of social services) was administered in each of the seven ecclesiastical districts of Rome in the seventh century by cardinals who were in the deacons' orders. This was "the last expression of the diaconate in its ancient form," since the basic trend in medieval Christendom was to separate the function of *diakonia* (service) from necessary relationship with the diaconate.[24]

Later medieval deacons assumed an increasingly ecclesiastical role, and their tendency to become candidates for the priesthood became more pronounced than ever. Almost no one was ordained to the diaconate unless he intended to advance to the priesthood. Thus, it was not surprising for cardinal deacons of Rome to be logical candidates for the papacy. Pope Innocent III took office in 1198 and administered church affairs for several weeks as a deacon before his ordination and consecration.[25]

Archdeacons (chief deacons) frequently became ecclesiastical justices of the peace and legal representatives of bishops. Thus, the archdeaconry became a political post, and this led at times to corruption. Geoffrey Chaucer, English poet of the fourteenth century, described certain archdeacons as those who, among other things, both "impose unlawful taxes upon the priests of their archdeacon-ries" and "suffer the clergy to live in their sins, for the sake of moneys which they extort from them." [26]

The Reformation Period

With the launching of the Protestant Reformation in the early sixteenth century, a new concept of the role and functions of deacons began to emerge. The Reformers, who "saw no great similarity between the ceremonial or political diaconate of the sixteenth century and that which they found in the New Testament," [27] vigorously asserted the need to recover New Testament patterns for deacons. The Reformers evidently made little provision for deaconesses as official church workers, although there are scattered references to them in Reformation literature. [28]

The Reformers moved away from the medieval emphases on the liturgical functions of deacons and on their advancement to the priesthood. Martin Luther claimed in 1520 that "the diaconate is the ministry, not of reading the Gospel or the Epistle, as is the present practice, but of distributing the church's aid to the poor." [29] Luther reestablished the crucial biblical link between deacons and *diakonia* (service). He further viewed deacons as a vital part of the laity rather than as a mere order of the priesthood.

Agreeing with Luther that the origin of deacons was in Acts 6, John Calvin, another leading Reformer, stated that "Scripture specifically designates as deacons those whom the church has appointed to distribute alms and take care of the poor, and serve as stewards of the common chest for the poor." [30] Calvin added, "Here, then, is the kind of deacons the apostolic church had, and which we, after their example, should have." [31] Calvin's ideas received concrete application in the Protestant church in Geneva, Switzerland. Two groups of deacons existed in this church. One group distributed charities, and the other served the sick.

The Continental Anabaptists, sometimes referred to as the radical wing of the Reformation in their stress on believer's baptism, and the English Separatists, who believed that true reformation could take place only by complete separation from the Church of England, provided immediate antecedents for the rise of Baptist deacons in the seventeenth century. A brief look at both groups is needed, especially at the English Separatists, who strongly influenced early Baptist practices.

Deacons were definitely a part of Anabaptist life. Jan Pauw suffered martyrdom at Amsterdam in the Netherlands on March 6, 1535, and was clearly identified as a deacon. About 1537 Ulrich Stadler of the Hutterites, Anabaptists who set up colonies in Moravia and Transylvania, defended the right of deacons to administer church discipline. A 1580 confession of faith of the Dutch Anabaptists implied that deacons were a vital part of church life. To be sure, "the early Anabaptist-Mennonite movement universally established the office of deacon as an important ordained office." [32]

Henry Barrow, a leader of the English Separatist movement between 1585 and 1593, had many things to say about deacons. In 1589 he described their duties as mainly gathering goods from the faithful members of the church and distributing these goods among the needy saints. He also urged deacons to ensure that proper provisions be made for other officers of the church. Barrow attacked what he considered to be misuses of the deacon's role. Observing that the bishop of Winchester believed deacons to be governing officers in the church, Barrow claimed that this was not a New Testament privilege of deacons and that, instead, "the deacon's office in the church is to gather and distribute." [33]

John Smyth, pastor of the Separatist congregation at Gainsborough, England, must be taken seriously concerning his views about deacons since in 1608-1609 in Amsterdam he was to become the founder and leader of the first Baptist congregation in history. As a Separatist, Smyth wrote in 1607 that deacons could be men or women. The chief duty of male deacons was to see that "none of the Saints want bodily necessaries, and that due provision be made for holy things and persons." [34] The primary duties of female deacons or widows, whom he classified together, were "to visit and relieve the widow, fatherless, sick, lame, blind, impotent, women with child, and diseased members of the church." [35] Smyth also said that deacons distributed the church's treasury to orphans, widows, the poor, and others.[36]

As a result of Reformation emphases, deacons eventually became a key part of many Christian denominations: Lutheran Church, Reformed Churches (including Presbyterianism), Mennonite churches, the Church of England, Congregational churches, Baptist churches, and others. The reason was a widespread affirmation of the centrality and value of deacons in the New Testament church.

Conclusion

Two sets of contrasting features characterized the diaconate of the early church and that of the Middle Ages. First, whereas deacons in the early church involved themselves in diverse ministries of practical Christian service, those in the Middle Ages isolated their work primarily to worship. Deacons of the first few centuries exercised significant roles in charitable visitation, benevolent activities, administration, teaching, preaching, evangelism, worship, counseling, living an exemplary life, and other ministries. The move away from this multiplicity of function to a narrower and mainly liturgical function helped lead to a decline in the diaconate which lasted until the Reformers of the sixteenth century sought to recover biblical ideals and practices for deacons.

Second, although the deacons in the early church interpreted their work basically in terms of service, those in the Middle Ages largely abandoned the ministry of *diakonia* in favor of a political climb up the bureaucracy of the clergy. Status and position took priority over function; New Testament concepts of the diaconate were abandoned; and the result was hundreds of years of diaconal weakness.

The Reformers challenged the excessive desire of deacons to

seek promotions in the ecclesiastical structure and put them back to work in a variety of service ministries. As a needed corrective, the Reformers made clear the New Testament teaching that the diaconate is a legitimate office in its own right. Anabaptists and English Separatists set the stage for the rise of Baptist deacons.

2

EARLY BAPTIST DEACONS

Deacons have been described in Baptist writings for well over 350 years. Baptists in England in the 1600s created many patterns for their deacons which were either imitated or paralleled by early Baptists in America. Early practices in America were then formative for the development of certain features of current deacon life.

Shaping Patterns Among English Baptists

The first Baptist to write about deacons was John Smyth, founder in 1608-1609 of the first Baptist church in history at Amsterdam in the Netherlands. As leader of the congregation, he claimed in 1609 that the church had the power to elect and ordain men and women to the diaconate and that the role of these deacons was to collect and distribute the monies of the church and to minister to its members.[1] Part of this congregation moved to England in 1611 under the leadership of Thomas Helwys and became the first Baptist church on English soil. Deacons were an integral part of English Baptist life from that point forward.

Several English Baptist pastors had some valuable things to say about deacons. In 1654 Thomas Collier described their work as that of serving tables—the table of the Lord, the table of the minister, and the table of the poor. They were also to edify the church with any spiritual gifts they had.[2]

In 1681 N. Cox stated in an ordination sermon that the special charge of deacons was to care for the poor. The contributions and alms of the church were to be deposited with and distributed

23

by them. Cox suggested four qualities for deacons as they carried out their charge: faithfulness, compassion, prudence, and diligence.

Cox showed the seriousness of the charge given to deacons in such assertions as "yea the poor Members of Christ, which are dear to him as the Apple of his Eye, are committed to your Care"; you cannot "relieve the Necessities of the poor Saints" unless you "do by a gracious Sympathy, as it were, put your selves in their stead"; besides being "full of wisdom," a deacon must "rightly discern of the Case and Circumstances of those that are to be relieved by him"; and "your Heart must be in your work." [3]

Cox also stressed the responsibilities of a congregation to its deacons. Church members were to respect them and to encourage them in their ministry. Cox strongly emphasized the need for a church to trust its deacons with its financial resources so that they could share them with the poor.[4]

In 1697 Elias Keach, a London pastor, claimed, as Thomas Collier had stated in 1654, that the work of deacons was to care for the tables of the Lord, the minister, and the poor. They were also to urge church members to contribute voluntarily and regularly to the church's ministries.[5]

Of prime importance is that in 1688 in Pennsylvania, Keach had become the first pastor of the Pennepack Church, formed the same year as the mother Baptist church of the Middle Colonies in America. Before returning to England in 1692, Keach's influence increased in America as he helped to organize three churches in New Jersey. Later, as a result of the impact he had on Baptist growth in the Middle Colonies, his writing of 1697 in which he described the work of deacons "was brought into unexpected prominence in America." [6] This process shows vividly how concepts of the work of deacons in seventeenth-century England probably influenced ideas about them in America.

The writings of individual Baptists in England in the 1600s reveal that deacons were a part of Baptist life from the outset, that ordination was the proper means of installing them into their office, that they were to perform a ministry of serving tables, that they were to receive and distribute a church's money, and that a church was to hold its deacons in esteem.

Most of the major confessions of faith of early English Baptists included statements about deacons. All the confessions which mentioned them cited New Testament passages as the authority for their existence and work. The confessions generally placed deacons among the officers of the church.

The very first Baptist confession was prepared in the Netherlands in 1609 by John Smyth. His statement, designed to represent the beliefs of his followers, spoke of deacons as those "ministers of the church . . . who attend to the affairs of the poor and sick brethren." [7]

Although written in Amsterdam, the confession prepared in 1611 by Thomas Helwys, soon afterward the pastor of the first Baptist congregation in England, became the first English Baptist confession. Article 20 described deacons as men and women who relieved the needs of the poor and the sick. They were to be elected and approved by their church with fasting, prayer, and the laying on of hands.[8] This was evidently the first and only major English Baptist confession of the 1600s to mention women deacons. Although Helwys' statement may or may not have described the actual existence of women deacons, it certainly approved the concept and appropriateness of them.

The London Confession of 1644 prompted one scholar to suggest that "perhaps no Confession of Faith has had so formative an influence on Baptist life as this one." [9] It grouped deacons among all the officers of the church whose inclusive role was the "feeding, governing, serving, and building up of his [Christ's] Church." [10]

The Standard Confession, signed by an assembly of Baptist leaders in 1660, referred to deacons as "overseers of the poor" through whose help church members were to make voluntary contributions sufficient to provide for the needs of "poor Saints belonging to the Church of Christ." [11] The General Assembly of General Baptists included a similar statement in their minutes of May 1697. Deacons were to collect contributions of church members, to observe who gave and how much, to "Admonish to more Liberalitie" those members who were "short" in their gifts, and to alert the church of any who refused to give more generously after being admonished so that "there may be an Equallity in performance of that great Duty." [12]

Early English Baptist confessions strongly stressed the right of each church to select its own deacons. Ordination was vital to setting them apart as church officers. The Helwys Confession of 1611 and the Orthodox Creed of 1678 included fasting in the ordination process. Four confessions, those of 1611, 1660, 1678, and the Second London Confession of 1677, which later became the basis of the important confession adopted by the Philadelphia Association in America in 1742, indicated that prayer and the laying on of hands were also crucial to ordination.[13]

Confessions differed little from the writings of individuals in their emphases concerning deacons. They identified deacons as church officers, approved ordination, related them especially to meeting the needs of the poor, involved them in the raising and spending of church money, and mentioned women deacons only rarely.

While confessions and pastors' writings tended to present ideals for deacons, church minutes reflected actual practices. In the records of six Baptist churches of the 1600s, five major themes about deacons appeared: selection and ordination, role in caring for the church's treasury, ministry to the sick and poor, discipline, and women in the diaconate.

Church minutes dealt more with the selection and ordination of deacons than any of the other themes. Churches used various procedures for electing deacons. One church elected a deacon in 1690 simply "by ye majority of voices." [14] Two other approaches included casting lots and using a single paper ballot.

Casting lots was evidently a common way of choosing deacons. English Baptists did not view this procedure as a matter of chance. Rather, they attached a theological significance to this means of selecting deacons. Casting lots was a way to allow God to make the ultimate choice.

The Warboys Church used this practice in 1647. In need of two deacons, the church at Fenstanton resorted to this approach in 1656 when its members were unable to obtain a large enough vote in favor of two men out of four who had been nominated. When the vote failed to produce two deacons, the elders of the church examined the four nominees to see if they could find any reason to disqualify any of them. After the elders were fully satisfied with all the nominees, the church decided to cast lots. They were made, prayer was offered that the Lord "would order and dispose of them," they were cast, and two of the four men quickly became deacons. Needing another deacon, the same church cast lots again in 1658 in order "to know which of those [nominated] were chosen by the Lord." [15]

How did the procedure for casting lots actually work? To illustrate, less than ten men were present on the day the Fenstanton Church needed to elect a deacon in 1658. After four men were nominated, only four remaining men were eligible to vote (women were not eligible to vote). Since there were so few, they chose to cast lots. Five lots were made. Four were blank, and one was marked. The reason was that all four nominees might receive blanks if it were God's desire that none of them should be selected. Prayer was made that the Lord would dispose of the lots according to his will. "After which the lots were given forth, and the first lot which was given forth was the lot which was no blank, which fell upon Will Yarle, who was then received as separated by the Lord." [16]

Further stressing the belief of early English Baptists that deacons could be chosen through any one of a number of different ways, the Broadmead Church in Bristol took even another approach.

This church gave advance notice to its members in 1680 that two deacons needed to be selected on a certain day. When that day came, the pastor explained to the church the qualifications and duties of deacons. The elders nominated six candidates. The church was to choose from among these or to nominate anyone else desired. When no further nominations were made, the six assented to their nomination and were asked to leave the room. Their names were placed on a single sheet of paper, and a straight line was drawn beside each name. Then each male member took a pen and "gave a stroke" beside the names of two nominees. "This course we took that every one might be free, silently, to pick who he was for, to avoid all prejudice that might otherwise happen." [17] Two men were chosen deacons by receiving adequate votes.

The records of only four of the six churches consulted had information about the ordination of deacons. Still, the basic thrust was that ordination was fundamental to the installation of new deacons. Various practices existed. Two churches included preparatory fasting, prayer, and the laying on of hands in their ordination procedures. A third church used prayer and the laying on of hands but made no mention of fasting. A fourth church used fasting and prayer in at least three ordination services but did not employ the laying on of hands. One man in this same church was set apart for his work as a deacon "upon trial" (probably an effort to implement the intention of 1 Tim. 3:10: "And let them also be tested first; then if they prove themselves blameless let them serve as deacons").[18]

Early English Baptist church records also dealt frequently with the role of deacons as caretakers of the church's treasury, thus suggesting that deacons have evidently been related to church finances since the beginnings of Baptist life. When John Thirwall became a deacon in the church at Hexham in 1652, "the church began a stock, putting it into his hand." When two deacons were ordained in the Broadmead Church in 1680, the pastor made clear to them that the church funds would be placed under their supervision and responsible, watchful guidance.[19]

Because of the role of deacons in church finances, some churches created ways to ensure that deacons were handling money properly. The Fenstanton Church adopted the proposal in 1652 that their deacons should give an account of the church monies at their disposal at least twice a year. This kind of audit check was also used by the church at Amersham.[20]

Deacons took the initiative to approach church members directly about the necessity of contributing money to help defray the expenses of the church. In 1690 the church at Ford "ordered that ye Deacons appear at the next Church meeting with the subscriptions & ye names of those yt [that] not subscribe."[21]

According to church records, deacons also ministered to the sick and distributed the church's funds to the poor. In 1693 the church at Ford "agreed . . . that the Deacon Bro: Tripp do take care of Bro: Wild in his sicknesse & administer Relief as is necessary."[22] To show that the deacons did not pass out a church's money at random but rather through a systematic and organized process, in 1652 the Fenstanton Church adopted a well-defined policy by which its deacons were to provide assistance to the needy.

The policy involved three steps. A person in need had to declare his or her condition to the church or its deacons. Then the deacons were to evaluate the need and share it with no less than two members of the church, one of whom had to be an elder. Last, the deacons were to offer financial help once the need was determined but never without the consent of at least two church members, one of whom again had to be an elder. One reason given for the second step in this policy was to prevent deacons from being "blamed for doing things according to their own mind." A reason given for the third step was "that the congregation may always know how their stock is laid out."[23] This whole policy illustrated that deacon authority was determined by the church and not by the deacons.

Another area of concern was the discipline of deacons for wrongfully assuming any kind of power. The constitution approved in 1675 by the Amersham Church stated that any deacons who tried to gain unacceptable authority would receive the sentence which "the Church shall Judg & the Lord by his word shall give." [24]

Deaconesses were mentioned in the minutes of only one church, but they were a key topic in those minutes; and the church was a prominent one. The Broadmead Church in Bristol appointed a deaconess in 1662, another in 1673 "upon trial," and three others in 1679. In all these instances, the women chosen were widows. The three set apart by fasting and prayer in 1679 were all described as being over sixty years old (based on 1 Tim. 5:9). The laying on of hands was not mentioned in any of these proceedings, and the services of setting apart deaconesses were probably not equivalent to full ordination.

Setting women apart to be deaconesses included three elements. The church requested and received from each woman a vow not to marry (based on 1 Tim. 5:11). A ruling elder then declared them to be deaconesses. Last, their duties were described to them. They were to visit the sick, provide for their needs, speak a word of support to them in order to strengthen their faith in Christ, and report to the elders and deacons special needs they discovered among the sick. In 1685 one of the deaconesses was admonished when the church agreed to send two members to her to "stir [her] up to her work, in visiting, &c., as a deaconess." [25]

To conclude this section, selected minutes of English Baptist churches in the 1600s revealed a number of important factors in the emerging role of deacons. Most of these factors were quite similar to early developments in America. Churches viewed the selecting of deacons as belonging mainly to God, especially in casting lots. Ordination was then the church's acknowledgment of God's choice and the giving of certain authority and privileges of ministry to deacons. Ordination was evidently confined to men in the diaconate.

Deacons related closely to money matters in churches through encouraging strong giving patterns, caring for money contributed, and using it particularly to aid the poor and sick. Deaconesses, too, had special ministries with the ill. Churches kept close watch over the diaconate and disciplined those in it who either exceeded their authority, failed to maintain high Christian standards, or refused to do their work of ministry.

Baptist Deacons in Early America

Evidence for the role and function of Baptist deacons in America in the 1600s is quite limited. To begin with, only a few Baptist churches were formed in America in this century. When the First Baptist Church of Philadelphia arose in 1698, it was apparently preceded by less than a dozen other churches.[26] Further, only a few limited records of these churches have been preserved. The records of the First Baptist Church of Boston, formed in 1665, and those of the Pennepack Church in Pennsylvania, founded in 1688, have been helpful. Deacons were definitely a part of Baptist life in these minutes, although there were apparently no references to deaconesses in Baptist church records in America in the 1600s.

At least three men served as deacons in the Boston Church in the 1600s. One of these was severely disciplined by the church in 1685 when he was discharged from his work as a deacon for "neglecting to officiate in his place for a long time and persisting in so doing." Another was elected in 1688 upon probation. A probationary period was evidently a common feature in the appointment of many early deacons. The Boston minutes also revealed that a deacon named Humphrey Churchwood was one of the ten signers of the covenant adopted by the Kittery Baptist Church at its formation in 1682 as the first Baptist church in Maine.[27] This was important because this church transplanted itself to Charleston, South Carolina, in the early 1680s, where it became the first Baptist church in the South and introduced deacons into the South.

At the time of its establishment in 1688, the Pennepack Church in Pennsylvania chose Samuel Vaus to be a deacon; and Elias Keach, the pastor, employed the laying on of hands during the ordination of Vaus. This was a clear example of English Baptist influence on deacon developments in America. Keach had grown up in England and returned to pastor a church there in the early 1690s.

The usual custom at the Pennepack Church during the Lord's Supper was for the deacon to receive the bread and cup from the pastor and to distribute them to the members. The deacon provided the bread and wine for the Supper from money gathered at the time of the previous celebration.[28] Thus, in the 1600s probationary election, ordination, discipline, and participation in the Lord's Supper were already a vital part of deacon life in America.

With the arrival of the eighteenth century, materials about deacons became more common. Prior to the 1770s, the basic sources for information about them were church minutes. After 1770 church and associational manuals, statements of discipline, and associational circular letters gave even more detailed data on them.

The ordination of deacons was practiced by Baptists in the North and South. The Newport Church in Rhode Island ordained two deacons in 1724. In 1737 a key element in the ordination of two others in the Ashley River Church in Charleston District, South Carolina, was a sermon based on 1 Timothy 3:13. Deacons even assisted in the ordination of ministers, as was done as early as 1711 in the Swansea Church in Massachusetts.[29]

Several important materials between 1742 and 1763 revealed the patterns in deacon progress. They showed further English Baptist influence; emphasized the ordination, ministry, and discipline of deacons; and began to relate deacons to the temporal affairs of church life, a trend which developed more fully in the last quarter of the century.

Adopted by the Philadelphia Association in 1742, the Philadelphia Confession was the most important Baptist statement of faith in America before the New Hampshire Confession of 1833. The Philadelphia Confession was based on the Second London Confession of 1677 and 1688 and continued the stress of the latter confes-

sion on the role of deacons as officers of the church and the ordination of deacons by prayer and the laying on of hands.[30]

A treatise on church order by Benjamin Griffith, which was published in conjunction with the Philadelphia Confession, stated that
deacons were to serve in the "outward concerns" of the church.
Having been "intrusted with the stock of the church," they were
to provide the elements for the Lord's Supper and to care for
the needs of the poor and the minister. Also, they were to encourage
all church members to contribute money for the needs of the
church.[31]

The Backus Memorial Baptist Church in North Middleboro, Massachusetts, came into being in 1756 as a Separate Baptist church
with the famous Isaac Backus as its pastor. The confession of faith
adopted by this church acknowledged the church's right to ordain
deacons and even to depose them if they walked contrary to the
gospel. Deacons in other places were subject to discipline too. In
1760 a deacon who had been disciplined by the Welsh Neck Church
in South Carolina confessed his sin publicly and sought the pardon
of the church. He then received back his membership privileges
"but continued suspended from his office as a deacon." The confession of Backus' church also asserted that deacons were to serve
the Lord's table, to care for the poor, and to oversee the church's
temporal affairs.[32]

The first deacon elected by the Backus Memorial Church was
Nathanael Shaw. His ordination in 1756 consisted of an examination by officers from another church, a sermon based on 1 Timothy
3:13 and a prayer by Isaac Backus, and a charge and final prayer
by an elder from another church. In 1758 this deacon was chosen
to assist Backus in ordaining two deacons in another church.[33]

One of the most detailed descriptions of a deacon ordination
in the eighteenth century appeared in the minutes of the First
Baptist Church of Philadelphia in 1763. The service began with
a prayer. Then a "dissertation" was delivered on the office, qualifications, duties, election, and installment of deacons. The pastor

received the three deacons-elect, laid his hands on them as they knelt, and prayed. His prayer mentioned four responsibilities of deacons: to collect the revenues of the church, to provide for and serve the Lord's table, to provide for the tables of the minister and the poor, and to transact other temporal concerns of the church. Finally, the three new deacons stood up from kneeling and received congratulations from the minister.[34]

In the latter half of the eighteenth century, a new concept of Baptist deacons emerged and continues to exist in many churches today. This was the view of deacons as church business managers. This view stressed to a seemingly excessive degree the administrative functions of deacons and tended to distract from other areas of service previously given equally strong attention. The concept appeared to a lesser extent in the already described minutes of the Backus Memorial Church and the Philadelphia Church in the idea that deacons should care for the temporal affairs of the churches while ministers should tend to the spiritual matters. Five documents prepared between 1773 and 1796 show even more clearly the rise of this trend.

A statement on church discipline which appeared in the 1773 minutes of the Welsh Tract Church in Delaware claimed that a basic duty of deacons was "to serve in the outward concerns of the church" and that the deacons, along with other church officers, were "the chief managers in the church." [35]

David Thomas, a leading Regular Baptist in Virginia, wrote in 1774 that part of the duty of a deacon was "to take care of the secular concerns of a church . . . and, in short, to be entrusted with all its temporal affairs." [36]

A treatise on church discipline published in 1774 by the Charleston Association in South Carolina stated that "the office of a deacon is to relieve the minister from the secular concerns of the church." [37]

Morgan Edwards was pastor of the Philadelphia Church from 1761 to 1771 and after that an evangelist for the Philadelphia Association and a compiler of several volumes of historical materials about Baptists in America. In 1774 he wrote that a deacon's office extends only to the secular affairs of a church, "obliging him to the due care and management thereof; authorizing him to require, receive, and lay out money towards answering the church's worldly necessities." In listing the work of deacons, Edwards placed at the head of the list "business." [38]

The 1796 circular letter of the Warwick Association in New York specified part of the work of a deacon as caring for the "temporalities of the Church." In referring to the role of deacons in the New Testament, the letter said that "the very office of a Deacon was to relieve the ministry, and not included in it." [39]

All of this is not to suggest that deacons in the late eighteenth century did not function in any capacity other than as church business managers. The evidence is plain that they engaged in other important areas of ministry and service. The general tendency was to divide the remaining work of deacons into serving tables, a theme which had persisted from the beginning of Baptist life.

Service to the Lord's table involved providing the bread and wine for the Lord's Supper, distributing the elements to the church members, admonishing those members who failed to attend the ordinance, and reporting to the church anyone who refused to heed such an admonition.

Service to the table of the poor involved encouraging members to contribute for benevolent purposes, distributing the church's funds to the poor, and taking particularly good care of needy widows.

Service to the table of the minister involved inspecting his needs and urging church members to provide him with the necessities of life. One association stated in a letter to its churches, "When deacons neglect this duty, they . . . prove the coldness of their love, and rob themselves and the Church in spiritual things." Another association believed so strongly in this duty that it asked its churches: "Are your Deacons neglectful in this matter . . . ?

Then you should displace them, and appoint others." [40]

Many deacons ministered well and lived sacrificial lives. Sampson Bryan, for example, was a deacon in the 1790s in an early black Baptist church in Savannah, Georgia. On account of his faith, he was imprisoned and whipped and suffered further persecution upon his release. In spite of the opposition, said one writer, "this good man never faltered" in his faith and "served the church faithfully until he fell asleep in Jesus early in the nineteenth century." [41]

Various records repeatedly urged that churches respect their deacons. According to the Charleston Association, churches were to "esteem them as being employed by the Lord to serve in the household of faith," "to submit to their godly and friendly admonitions," and "to encourage them by cheerful and liberal contributions for the service of God's house, his ministers, and his poor." [42]

The eighteenth-century writing which apparently gave more information about deacons than any other was Morgan Edwards' *The Customs of Primitive Churches* (1774). Although designed to be a manual of the polity and practices of the churches in the Philadelphia Baptist Association, the writing was never officially adopted by this association. Still, because Edwards was such a prominent Baptist leader and because his statements about deacons were so similar to other statements during the period, his writing likely reflected a widespread opinion about deacons, even though only a few copies were ever printed.

Edwards claimed that the proper and biblical elements in a deacon ordination were a meeting of the congregation, evidence of fasting, a prayer, the selection of the men to be ordained, the acceptance of the nominations by the men chosen, an examination of the faith and intentions of these men by the ministers present, the laying on of hands, a prayer, a charge, an offer of the right hand of fellowship, the kiss of charity, a commendatory prayer, praise, and the benediction. [43]

Edwards then presented an elaborate account of an actual ordination service consisting of these parts. [44] Although he did not indicate the source of this account, it could easily have evolved out of his personal experience as pastor of the Philadelphia Church from 1761 to 1771. Three details of this service deserve special mention.

To begin with, the comments and opening prayer of the presiding minister emphasized certain aspects of deacon work. Along with taking good care of the poor, they were to care generally "for the bodily necessities of his [Christ's] saints," while the minister was to concern himself with "the necessities of their souls."

Next, the procedure for selecting deacons was for each male church member to cast a written ballot nominating two men whom he believed to be worthy of the diaconate. Of the men nominated, the two receiving the majority of votes were made the deacons.

Last, the service concluded with the singing of a hymn about deacons. Each of the first four stanzas reflected a different function of deacons. They were to care for the Lord's table, the poor, the minister, and strangers and other temporal matters. These duties were common expectations which Baptists in America had of their deacons in the 1600s and 1700s. The last stanza then encouraged deacons to adore Christ and implore his blessings on their work. Because of the rarity of a hymn about deacons, especially one that is over two hundred years old, the stanzas appear here in full:

> The temple of the Lord are we
>   His table here he hath,
> Which deacons serve, and serving, see
> Themselves advanc'd to good degree;
>   And boldness in the faith.
>
> The poor behold their father's care
>   To find them daily bread;
> For them the caring deacons are
> Both food and raiment to prepare;
>   And where to lay their head.
>
> Ye priests! whose office spreadeth wide
>   The deacons are for you,
> Your table comforts to provide,
> And help you in your work beside;
>   Your double thanks are due.

> The church's temporals, and store
>   The deacons well attend;
> The pious stranger needs no more
> Lodge at the inn; nor out of door;
>   For deacons are his friend.
>
> Let stranger, church, and priest, and poor,
>   And deacons join in one
> Their dearest Saviour to adore;
> And needful blessings to implore
>   On all we now have done.[45]

In several writings dated between 1770 and 1774, Morgan Edwards gave what were apparently the most detailed descriptions of Baptist deaconesses in America in the 1700s. He favored deaconesses and identified Romans 16:1 and 1 Timothy 3:11 as biblical bases for them. He said that he could offer no account of an actual ordination of a deaconess because one had never come to his attention. Still, he personally believed that deaconesses should be ordained. His belief at this point was obviously a minority opinion among the Baptists of his day. In describing their work, Edwards wrote that they were to nurse the sick, tend to the poor, and confine themselves "chiefly . . . to those things wherefor men are less fit." [46]

Deaconesses in the eighteenth century was confined largely to the Separate Baptists. In his travels up and down the eastern states, Edwards located deaconesses in nine Separate Baptist churches in Virginia, three in North Carolina, and one in South Carolina. He also found them in a few Particular (Calvinistic) Baptist churches in South Carolina and in a few Tunker (German) Baptist churches in Pennsylvania.[47]

Two factors may have helped to account for the increase in the number of deaconesses, especially among the Separate Baptists, in the latter 1700s. For one thing, the Great Awakening coupled with the mounting concern for liberty in America may have encouraged equality between men and women through the stress on individual duties and privileges.

Also, the Sandy Creek Church in North Carolina had deacon-esses. Formed in 1755 as the mother church of the Separate Baptists in the South, this church may have influenced the spread of deaconess developments. By 1772 it had become the mother, grandmother, and great-grandmother of forty-two other churches from which had come 125 ministers.[48]

Conclusion

Several important principles emerge from the history of early Baptist deacons in England and America. First, deacons received their authority from God, the New Testament, and the local church. A church did not view the casting of lots as pure chance but as a time for God to be actively involved in the selection of deacons. Baptists regularly appealed to the New Testament in defending the existence and defining the qualifications and role of deacons. A church ordained deacons, using prayer, the laying on of hands, and fasting as means of giving authority to deacons.

Second, the authority given to deacons was for positive and practical purposes—namely, to serve as church officers, to assist in limited administrative functions, to care for a church's treasury, to make adequate provisions for the Lord's table, to ensure that the minister's needs were cared for, to minister to the sick, to stimulate responsible stewardship by encouraging voluntary contributions, and to be general servants of God, the church, and the needy.

Third, because deacons were given authority by the church, they were also responsible to the church. This responsibility often manifested itself in a probationary period following a deacon's election and in the examination of the candidate and the laying on of hands employed in ordination. To ensure that deacons lived upright lives and did not misuse their authority or the money entrusted to them, churches developed organized procedures by which deacons were to distribute financial aid. The church members required deacons at regular intervals to give account of their use of the church's money and disciplined deacons when they overextended their authority or engaged in a wayward pattern of life.

Fourth, in America in the latter half of the eighteenth century, the role of deacons as caretakers of the temporal or secular affairs of the church began to assume a priority that it had never had before. The involvement of deacons in administrative, managerial, and business functions became more pronounced. As churches became more numerous, pastors served more than one church and could spend only a limited amount of time doing administrative work in each. Thus, deacons did this work. Because church committee structures were not as developed as they are today, deacons were the logical persons to perform administrative tasks.

Last, although there were a few Baptist deaconesses in the period under consideration, they generally were not ordained. While some Baptists believed there was sufficient biblical evidence to justify their existence, most did not. The churches which did favor deaconesses normally did not lay hands on them but simply set them aside with prayer and, occasionally, fasting, to minister to the sick, to the poor, and particularly to women.

3

MODERN BAPTIST DEACONS

Evidence for the role and functions of Baptist deacons in America became increasingly widespread in the nineteenth and twentieth centuries. Basically, the literature of the 1800s continued most of the themes about deacons from the 1700s, including an expanded emphasis on deacons as church business managers. Deacon bodies were described as boards as early as the 1840s.

One new theme that emerged was a negative reaction to the idea of deacons as boards whose primary work was to care for church business. Much of the literature in the twentieth century has also expressed this new theme and has even moved beyond it by pointing to positive ways that deacons can balance their work with a variety of helping ministries. The momentum of this new thrust developed gradually until a rapid acceleration began about 1950. Acceptance of deaconesses grew slowly and experienced decline somewhat in the 1800s and early 1900s but has become more widespread in recent years.

The Nineteenth Century

Associational circular letters, church manuals, and miscellaneous writings by Baptist pastors, professors, and others were read widely by Baptists and strongly influenced deacon developments in churches. The main content of all these sources was capsulized in the New Hampshire Confession of Faith of 1833, which was probably the most common confession among Baptists in America in the 1800s. Asserting that the church's "only proper officers are

Bishops or Pastors, and Deacons," [1] this confession placed deacons squarely within its definition of the leadership of churches.

Eight representative associational letters of Baptists in the North and South and dating from 1804 to 1850 provided a good summary of associational interpretations of the role of deacons.[2] These letters repeated the thrust of eighteenth-century sources which divided deacons' main duties into meeting the needs of the table of the Lord, the table of the poor, and the table of the minister. Other specific assignments included urging members to contribute money for the work of the church, admonishing delinquent members to fulfill their duties, assisting the pastor in settling differences among members, attending church meetings, caring for the afflicted, and teaching other members.

These letters gave particular stress to the business aspects of deacons' work. Various letters said that deacons were to serve as trustees, to manage the church's secular and temporal affairs, to assess, collect, and disburse the church's funds, and to be "second in command" to the pastor in these and related matters.

The 1842 letter of the Salem Association in Massachusetts advocated an early system of rotating terms for deacons. The letter proposed that rather than be elected for life, as was the usual custom, deacons should be elected for a limited time of office. Among the reasons cited were that the church could regularly have the services of the best men and that the work of the pastor and the church would be enhanced. In this proposed approach deacons were to be eligible for reelection.

Associational circular letters were a vital means of communication among Baptists, especially in the period before Baptist state newspapers appeared. The letters reflected the thinking of groups of churches about deacons. Further, since they have been described as "an engine of immense power" and as "the molding force . . . which in the early days of associational life was unexcelled," [3] their statements on deacons likely helped to determine the character of the diaconate among Baptists in America in the first half of the 1800s, thus influencing our contemporary concepts.

Dozens of Baptist church manuals were published in America in the 1800s. They,' too, both reflected and influenced the polity and practice of churches at the time they were written. Originally published between 1845 and 1867, hundreds of thousands of four of these manuals have been sold. William Crowell's *The Church Member's Manual* (1845) went through six printings by 1873. J. Newton Brown's *The Baptist Church Manual* (1853) received twenty-two printings by 1957. By 1894 about 60,000 copies of Edward T. Hiscox's *The Baptist Church Directory* (1859) had been circulated. By 1946 about 150,000 copies of J. M. Pendleton's *Church Manual* (1867) had been printed.[4] These manuals made a significant impact on deacon developments in churches throughout the country.

On the election of deacons, the manuals agreed that they should be chosen by a free vote of the church and should be selected from among the faithful and experienced members. The number of deacons should hinge on the discretion and needs of the individual congregation. Most of the manuals claimed that deacons should be appointed for an indefinite tenure, but Crowell believed that in some instances there might be reasons for limiting a term of service. He cited such factors as failing mental or physical health, a decline in spirituality, and the appearance of more qualified men in the church.[5]

The manuals were at one in viewing ordination, including prayer and the laying on of hands, as the proper way to set deacons apart for their office. Brown urged that an ordination be preceded by one year's trial. Hiscox lamented that the ordination of deacons was not practiced as widely in some parts of the country as it had previously been. He asserted that a recovery of the practice would both add a higher esteem to the office and help guarantee the biblical character of the diaconate.[6]

General duties ascribed to deacons by the manuals included assisting in baptism and the Lord's Supper, taking the alms of the church to the poor members, visiting the sick, ensuring that the minister was properly compensated, conducting meetings for prayer, and aiding the pastor in the basic performance of his tasks.

On the matter of diaconal involvement in handling church business, Brown and Hiscox, without going into detail, simply indicated that deacons should provide general supervision for the "temporal" affairs of the church. Pendleton related deacons to the business end of a church in a rather extensive way. Since he was an important leader in the Landmark movement, which exerted an enormous influence on Southern Baptist life, the popularity of his manual made a distinct impact on Southern Baptists.

Pendleton even went to the extreme of claiming that deacons should be both the treasurers and trustees of churches. He attempted to add scriptural validity to his distinction between the spiritual duties of pastors and the secular duties of deacons by quoting Acts 6:3-4, which says, "Wherefore, brethren, look ye out among you seven men . . . whom we may appoint over this business. But we will give ourselves continually to prayer, and to the ministry of the word" (KJV).[7] Pendleton possibly made a strong connection between deacons and the word "business" (v. 3). Also, he apparently viewed this "business" as church management, when the biblical intent was for the seven to "serve tables" (v. 2).

Pendleton's concept of deacon work cannot be underestimated in terms of its influence on Baptists in America, especially since his manual of 1867 is still in print. He gave substantial impetus to the existing tendency of many writers to make a sharp separation between deacons and spiritual ministries. This trend, which converted the deaconship into church business management, represented a marked departure from the New Testament idea of deacons as ministers of practical service. While doing church business is a ministry, it is not the primary function of deacons. The Bible and church history call for a fuller participation of deacons in meeting the basic needs of hurting humanity.

Miscellaneous writings of the 1800s shared general information about deacons, amplified further on the management function of deacons, and presented negative reactions to the increasing role of deacons in church business. General information was varied. One church regularly appointed "junior deacons," or trainees, who served alongside "senior deacons." Another appointed black deacons to serve its black members. Several writers believed that deacons should be appointed for limited terms rather than for life. As churches became larger and the memberships more diverse, this seemed an appropriate way for them to make sure that they had the best leadership at all times. One writing urged pastors to resist firmly but affectionately the election to the diaconate of any man who did not possess proper biblical qualifications. Another applied church discipline to deacons in saying that the power of a church to make a man a deacon was also sufficient to displace him as a deacon if he proved himself unworthy or unfaithful.[8]

In 1840 Hosea Holcombe, historian of Alabama Baptists, printed a beautiful poetic statement which focused on the urgent need for deacons to support their ministers. A part of this statement appears here because of the excellent way it portrays the persisting call in Baptist historical literature for deacons to serve the table of the minister. Also, this statement has an undeniable contemporary relevance in its emphasis on the need for deacons to support the effective preaching of the gospel.

> Deacons awake, good counsel take;
>   Arise from sluggish sleeping;
> Stand to your post, and prove your trust,
>   For ministers are weeping.
>
> They're called to teach, and you to preach;
>   And ought to be maintained;
> They have to go through floods of woe,
>   And you are to be blamed.
>
> Come lay by sloth, and venture forth,
>   To call the congregation,
> For to support the Gospel work,
>   And spread abroad salvation.

> Come loose the hands of those who stand,
>   Up to declare a Saviour;
> On you 'tis laid to give them aid,
>   And shew them love and favour.
>
> Relieve their wants, hear their complaints,
>   And let them go on preaching;
> On you it rests to make them bless'd,
>   And give them constant teaching.[9]

The role of deacons in the business affairs of church life received considerable attention by many writers. Perhaps the most influential was R. B. C. Howell, pastor of the First Baptist Church of Nashville, Tennessee, and editor of *The Baptist,* a Baptist newspaper. In 1846 he published his book *The Deaconship.* As one of the most detailed books ever written on Baptist deacons up to that time, Howell's writing was destined to exert a significant impact on deacon trends. The book has been so popular that Judson Press published the eleventh printing in 1977.

Designating deacons as "the financial officers of the church," Howell also referred to them as "a BOARD OF OFFICERS, or the *executive board* of the church, for her temporal department." [10] His descriptions of deacons as a "board" both here and at other places in his book perhaps comprised the earliest applications of this term to deacons in Baptist literature. Through his concept of deacons as a board, Howell ascribed to them heavy responsibilities in church business management. He believed, for example, that all church property and funds should be placed under their direction.[11]

In addition to their role in financial promotion and management, deacons were to care for other "temporal" matters, such as making sure the church building was comfortable, preparing the baptismal pool, arranging the furniture for the Lord's Supper, and making certain that the needs of visiting pastors and evangelists were met.[12]

Howell did not give unlimited authority to deacons. He claimed both that "it is not . . . the duty of the deacons to rule the church" and that diaconal authority "is not absolute, but limited to such uses as the church may order." [13]

Although Howell viewed church business matters as a key concern of deacons, he also stressed some complementary and traditional forms of diaconal ministry which he considered essential. Deacons were to care for "the wants of the poor, the distressed, the afflicted, the fatherless, and the widows of the household of faith, and especially of their own particular church." Furthermore, he wrote, "Much visiting by the deacons will, I apprehend, be found positively indispensable." [14]

Other writers took the same position as Howell in assigning many business functions to deacons. In 1846 William Bullein Johnson, first president of the Southern Baptist Convention, listed a "capacity for business" as an imperative qualification for deacons. In describing the "departments of service" in the deaconship, three of the four he mentioned were business related—serving as church treasurer, as church clerk, and as supervisor of the church building and its furnishings. Another writer claimed in 1897 that deacons should "possess good executive ability," since they are largely in charge of "the management of all financial matters in the church." [15]

By the middle of the nineteenth century, the view of deacons as church business managers was becoming increasingly obvious in many important writings. Several prominent Baptists became alarmed at this trend and at the extreme amounts of authority which deacons were assuming in some places. As a result, in the latter half of the 1800s they began to oppose the concept of deacon bodies as boards and the confining of deacon work more and more to the secular affairs of the church.

In 1852 Thomas Armitage, a pastor/historian in New York, attacked the idea which he said was being entertained in his day that a deacon was a person "of so much importance and ecclesiastical consequence in the Church, that all the membership, and all the affairs in the Church, and the Pastor, must be dictated, and ruled, and governed by him." [16] In contrast, Armitage stressed the pastoral dimension of the deaconship and encouraged a great deal of pastoral visitation by deacons.

John L. Dagg, Mercer University professor until 1856, wrote in his retirement that deacons should promote the "spiritual interests of the church" and were not released from this obligation "by their appointment to minister in secular affairs." In 1877 Alvah Hovey, Baptist theologian, challenged the idea that deacons should be in charge of church finances, stated that a church treasurer did not need to be a deacon, and even suggested that a finance committee could look after matters relating to money.[17]

Edwin C. Dargan, professor of homiletics and ecclesiology at Southern Baptist Theological Seminary, launched perhaps the most powerful attack against the trend in question. In 1897 he wrote of a danger which he saw to be inherent in the tendency for deacons to act as "a sort of ruling presbytery." Then he spoke of the growing pattern "to speak of the deacons as a 'board,' or sometimes even as an 'official board,' and to consider them in some sort the representatives and governors of the churches." [18]

Dargan believed that one cause of this dangerous trend was the occasional, unwarranted assumption of power by deacons themselves. The more probable cause, in his opinion, lay with the members themselves rather than with the deacons. "Our church members neglect too much the business meetings of the church. They turn over the business of the church too readily and easily to the deacons to perform for them." Dargan recommended both a renewed respect for the office of deacon and a recovery of "the proper scriptural functions of the diaconate." [19]

By the end of the 1900s, two opposing views of the nature and function of the diaconate had forceful proponents in Baptist life. There seemed to be no easy resolution to the differences, especially since advocates of both sides appealed to the New Testament as the foundation for their beliefs. The stage was thus set for continuing discussion of the two contrasting approaches in the present century.

Another point about which nineteenth-century Baptist writers expressed conflicting opinions was the acceptability of deaconesses. A sampling of the views of some major writers shows a variety of stances on the topic. R. B. C. Howell (1846) saw no biblical basis for ordaining deaconesses but still believed that "Apostolic example authorizes and enjoins their appointment." William Bullein Johnson (1846) stated that they could be "particularly useful" in certain functions. William Williams (sometime between 1859 and 1877) of the Southern Baptist Theological Seminary considered them "unnecessary." Edward T. Hiscox (1894) favored them. E. C. Dargan (1897) wrote that 1 Timothy 3:11 did not make deaconesses obligatory, but because of this trace of biblical authority "there would be no objection to establishing it [the deaconess office] should it be found expedient and clearly promotive of good so to do." [20]

Whatever the beliefs of prominent Baptist writers about deaconesses, there were comparatively few women in this role in Baptist life in the 1800s. Available data seems to suggest a decline in the number of deaconesses in certain places and times during this century. A book on church polity asserted in 1849 that deaconesses had "fallen into desuetude," and Edward T. Hiscox wrote in 1894 that only "a few churches retain the practice." [21] One reason for the decline was the narrowing of the diaconal function more and more to business and management categories. The combination of this trend with the American tendency to place men in management positions in all phases of society had predictable consequences for the deaconess concept.

The Twentieth Century

The tendency to involve deacons significantly in handling church business concerns continued into the twentieth century. After describing deacons as the "pastor's cabinet," one writer asserted that "all matters of large import should come to the church by recommendation of the deacons." P. E. Burroughs made clear in his widely read study course book, *Honoring the Deaconship*, that deacons should be responsible for church finances. A Primitive Baptist stated in a similar vein, "It is the duty of the Deacons at the beginning of each church year to do what the directors of any other business or corporation would do; that is, take stock to find their assets and liabilities." The *Encyclopedia of Southern Baptists* claimed as recently as 1958, "Although Baptist polity permits a wide latitude of form and practice, the deacon usually renders an administrative and officiating ministry." [22]

In reaction to these continuing trends, other writers in the first half of the 1900s stressed three themes. First, they frowned upon the idea of deacons being too closely aligned with church business. W. T. Conner, theology professor at Southwestern Baptist Theological Seminary, believed that deacons, following biblical qualifications, should strive for spiritual objectives in all their work and that "no man should be made a deacon merely because he is a good business man." Gaines S. Dobbins, noted religious educator, stated, "A deacon . . . is not merely a business officer of the church. He is a specially qualified man of God called by his church to high and holy spiritual service." Another writer said that "too many churches seem willing to allow the deacons to shoulder the entire responsibility for the business affairs which claim attention." [23]

The second theme consisted of cautions against the misuse of authority by deacons. One writer related the issue of deacon authority to small rural churches. He pointed to the temptation in these churches for certain "overbearing" deacons to develop "unlovely traits of assertiveness of opinion and assumption of authority" and believed that these traits had helped in many instances to bring the diaconate into disrepute. [24]

In an important book Frederick A. Agar related deacon authority to ordination and to the duration of a deacon's term of office.

He believed the ordination of deacons to be a dangerous practice because "it leads many people to wrong conclusions concerning the import of a setting-apart service." This led him to feel that the laying on of hands was not essential.[25] Agar's book, published by Judson Press of the then Northern Baptist Convention, was likely a factor behind the present widespread custom of not ordaining deacons in the American Baptist Churches in the United States. Southern Baptist churches continue to ordain deacons by using the laying on of hands.

Agar also believed that a deacon should not hold office for a life term because of the occasional tendency to urge his own will over the will of the church. This tendency had grown in some churches to the extent that "one finds the board of deacons in absolute and final control of the affairs of the church, and this without any constitutional right." [26]

One writer said that deacons were not to think of themselves as the church, to view themselves as a board, or to presume to move ahead of the church. Two other writers accepted the term "board of deacons" but warned against illegitimate uses of authority issuing from such a board. The warning was given that the nature and function of the deacon's office is misunderstood when a board of deacons is considered "the equivalent of a 'Board of Directors' and all officers of the church (including the pastor) are responsible to the 'Board.' " A similar caution said that for a board of deacons to exercise the authority of the church was "absolutely contrary to Baptist usage and principles" and that deacons could act only in an advisory capacity to the church in business matters.[27]

A third emphasis of writers in the first half of the twentieth century was that deacons have spiritual duties to perform other than those related to church business and the ordinances. Specific ministries listed included setting an example, providing for the poor, caring for the pastor's needs, calling on the sick, visiting the troubled, shepherding the congregation, evangelizing, preaching, and more.

Walter Rauschenbusch, an important Baptist leader of the Social Gospel movement early in the century, believed that many deacons had become so preoccupied with serving the Lord's Supper and managing church affairs that they had lost sight of other forms of ministry. He urged deacons to continue these basic types of service but to use initiative in searching for additional kinds of important work yet to be done. As one possibility, he suggested that deacons could seriously begin to grapple with problems of poverty.[28]

Deacons in many churches approached their spiritual tasks vigorously. For example, by 1915 the Judson Memorial Baptist Church in lower New York had developed several social ministries, such as a free clinic to help the sick. One writer said about this church that "here the office of deacon is no figurehead affair. It stands for downright work. The passing of the cup is but an incident of solid weeks of ministration over a wide range of need." [29]

This same writer stressed the values he saw in a particular way by which deacons in some churches were beginning to accomplish spiritual ministries. This was the plan of dividing the church membership into groups with one deacon responsible for ministering to each group. "In this way cases of sickness can be easily reported; the systematic visitation of the membership can be carried out and the social unity of the church built up." [30] This was obviously an early form of a deacon family ministry plan.

Several Southern Baptist churches had deaconesses between 1900 and 1950. An example was the Forks of Elkhorn Church in Kentucky which elected a number of them, along with "junior deaconesses," in 1921. John R. Sampey, pastor of the church and professor at the Southern Baptist Theological Seminary, divided the congregation into groups and suggested the election of deaconesses who could help minister to these groups. In their installation service the deaconesses were given an "earnest charge" rather than the laying on of hands in formal ordination.[31]

A church manual largely representing practices among Northern

Baptists reported in 1935 that "an increasing number of churches parallel the board of deacons with a board of deaconesses." [32]

The early twentieth century witnessed a deepening of the struggle between the board concept of deacons, including more authority for them in vital areas of church business management, and the concept which encouraged more participation by them in the pastoral ministries of the church. Existing side by side, each view had considerable strength. How to help churches determine which view had a more solid biblical basis and then to implement that view in practical action would become the primary agenda of post-1950 writings on deacons.

Very little time elapsed before one of these views began to assume priority. Writings about deacons since 1950 distinctly reveal an acceleration of the tendency to suggest multiple caring ministries for deacons and to deny the value of their engaging too extensively in church business. Gaines S. Dobbins struck a keynote in 1951 when he stated that deacons are "servants of the church, never managers or dictators." [33]

Robert E. Naylor was equally forceful when he wrote in 1955 in *The Baptist Deacon* that among the deacons in many churches a certain " 'bossism' has developed. There is a 'board' complex and a general feeling that deacons are 'directors' of the church. Nothing could be farther from the Baptist genius or the New Testament plan." [34] Naylor then described valuable ministries which deacons could perform in addition to those related to church business.

Two further events in the 1950s contributed in an important way to deacon developments. To begin with, the Deacon-led Spiritual Growth Program was launched among Southern Baptists by their Sunday School Board. This program stressed the spiritual ministries of deacons. Based on a division of church membership into family groups for which deacons were responsible, the program involved deacon visits to new converts, to new members who came by letter or statement, and to families already in the church.[35] Also, *Church Administration* was initially published in 1959 by the

Sunday School Board. This periodical frequently contained articles encouraging deacons to share in a variety of ministries.

The 1960s saw the publication of two helpful books on deacons by Judson Press of the American Baptist Convention. Entitled *The Work of the Deacon and Deaconess,* the first advocated diaconal involvement in many forms of practical service. Entitled *The Deacon in a Changing Church,* the other urged modern deacons to be courageous in their commitment to Jesus Christ and to be flexible in their efforts to meet new challenges and opportunities for ministry.[36]

In the 1960s Southern Baptists produced several important items which accented pastoral ministries for deacons. The Church Administration Department of the Sunday School Board published both a series of pamphlets under the general title "The Deacon Sets an Example" and a separate pamphlet entitled "Deacons in Training." The latter emphasized the training of deacons for participation in pastoral ministries, such as personal witnessing and helping persons in times of crisis. Retreats were suggested as places where deacons could study these subjects in detail.

Most important, in 1968 Convention Press published Howard B. Foshee's book *The Ministry of the Deacon,* of which more than 200,000 copies have been printed. Foshee reacted against the concept of deacons as a "board of directors by whom all major recommendations of church organizations and committees are screened before going to the congregation, to whom the pastor and staff are directly responsible, and by whom expenditures of major church resources should first be approved." [37] He also opposed the idea of deacons as a "board" whose sole duties are the management of business matters, who administer church affairs basically as a business operation, whose image is that of decision makers in all business affairs, and for whom business efficiency is a higher priority than Christian growth and service.[38]

In contrast, Foshee focused at length on the emerging role of deacons in the pastoral ministries of the church. These ministries included witnessing, preaching, counseling, benevolence, worship, education, community projects, and others.[39] Foshee thus placed deacons alongside pastors as ministers to the spiritual needs of people. His emphasis on the pastoral ministries of deacons has made a definite impact on Southern Baptists in their search for a more adequate concept of deacon service. Foshee's book is basic to understanding the current Deacon Family Ministry Plan, serves as a text for a flourishing church study course on deacon ministries, and is a vital part of the study materials in the modular unit of study "Deacons Training to Minister," which is integral to the Leadership Equipping Center of the Church Training Department of the Sunday School Board.

The 1970s witnessed several exciting innovations for Southern Baptist deacons. In October 1970 the first issue of *The Deacon* was published by the Church Administration Department of the Sunday School Board. The editor stated in that issue that the periodical was established because no other periodical spoke directly to deacons, because of its potential value as a training tool for deacons, and because deacons needed a regular source of information for understanding their role.

The editor expressed regret that deacons had dealt mainly with administrative concerns and business matters for too long and that in some churches they "even operate as a 'board of directors,' acting for the church in matters of policy and finance." After stating that "too many deacons have missed the joy of dealing directly with people in a ministry of care and compassion," he asserted that "the time has come for deacons to get involved in a spiritual ministry to human needs." He then claimed that as a means of helping deacons become more effective Christian servants, *"The Deacon* will give regular, detailed attention to the deacon's role as a servant and spiritual 'minister' in the church and community." [40] The popularity and influence of this publication can be partially measured by the fact that the circulation has increased to about 100,000 copies per quarter.

In 1972 the Church Administration Department introduced the

Deacon Family Ministry Plan, an outgrowth of the earlier Deacon-led Spiritual Growth Program and its successor, the Deacon Family-Care Plan. In this plan church membership was divided into family units, with each deacon having responsibility for a certain number of families. All deacons were to develop a visitation ministry to their families. They were to share the gospel with them, care for them, help them have a rewarding church membership, and guide them in building constructive community relationships.[41]

Over 20 percent of all Southern Baptist churches have adopted the Deacon Family Ministry Plan.[42] A key person behind the success of the plan has been Charles Treadway, who for several years has served as the national consultant in deacon ministry for the Sunday School Board. His *Deacon Chairman Planning Guide* was released by Convention Press in 1978. In addition, the Sunday School Board has produced a variety of other materials designed to help deacons minister more effectively to families.

The thrust of recent literature on deacons is clear. The accent is on deacon ministries. The comments of John F. Havlik beautifully epitomize the current thrust. He says, "The first deacons were not an official board formed to conduct church business. They were men who were to be models of ministry for the whole congregation." After commending the Deacon Family Ministry Plan, Havlik concludes that for each family in a church under the caring role of a deacon, "the deacon is their minister. He awakens in them the desire to minister." [43]

In his book of December 1980, *Deacons: Servant Models in the Church* (Convention Press), Henry Webb carefully develops the modeling role of deacons in several vital areas: growth toward mature faith, personal and public morality, Christian family life, active church involvement, ministry to persons, care for families, proclamation of the gospel, and church leadership. The purpose of this book is to train deacons to demonstrate in their lives and apply in their church the biblical concepts of their role as church leaders.

Deacons in thousands of churches are implementing the thrust toward creative ministries and are experiencing positive shifts in their roles. One solid illustration, among hundreds of possible examples, is the Hominy Baptist Church in Candler, North Carolina, which formed a Deacon Economic Assistance Committee (DEAC) to assist church members afflicted with economic problems.[44]

Along with other developments among deacons in the 1970s, the role of women in the diaconate has experienced a renewed interest. Contributing causes have included the women's rights movement and the tendency to view the diaconate as a comprehensive approach to pastoral ministries rather than as a more narrowly focused means of doing church business management, from which women have largely been excluded in the Baptist past.

Publications have also been influential factors. *The Broadman Bible Commentary* favors the meaning "deaconess" in its discussion of Romans 16:1 and concludes that the weight of evidence "slightly" favors the meaning "deaconess" in 1 Timothy 3:11. Long before that, A. T. Robertson, probably the most renowned New Testament scholar in Southern Baptist life in the twentieth century, influenced many in claiming that both of these verses apparently referred to women deacons.[45]

Other causes for the renewed interest, suggested by Leon McBeth, noted Baptist historian who teaches at Southwestern Baptist Theological Seminary, include changes in society, such as better education and new options for women outside the home; the example of other denominations; new understandings of biblical teachings; an increased depth in historical research; and practical considerations, such as the recognition that females comprise over half the membership and attendance of the typical church and that women are in the forefront of many church programs.[46]

Evidence for the new interest in women deacons is easy to find. Several churches elected women to the diaconate in the 1970s. Women have even been elected as chairpersons of the deacon bodies in a few churches. The actual number of women in deacon roles also helps to confirm the new interest. Virginia alone reported

520 in fifty-seven churches in 1976. There are possibly a few thou-
sand in Southern Baptist life today, many of whom are ordained;
but most are in churches in the Southeast. Major articles and related
writings further support the new interest in women deacons.[47]

Still, the electing of women to the deaconship exists in only a
small minority of Southern Baptist churches. A key reason is the
influence of certain Southern Baptist Bible scholars who claim that
there is insufficient biblical evidence to support women deacons.
Frank Stagg, noted New Testament Greek scholar and theologian,
wrote in a widely read book that "Evidence is too scant to determine
whether or not the reference [1 Timothy 3:11] . . . is to deaconesses or to the wives of deacons." [48] More recently, Stagg and
his wife, in a joint book, wrote about Romans 16:1 that although
the verse affirms the partnership of women in church work, "This
passage cannot be used as a proof text clinching the argument
for women 'deacons.' " [49]

Southern Baptist churches with women in the diaconate have
various practices regarding them. Some churches ordain them;
some do not. Some churches have given them equality of role,
status, and responsibility with male deacons and, depending on
the church, have designated them either "deaconesses" or "women
deacons." Other churches have given women in the diaconate a
lesser role, status, and responsibility than male deacons and have
usually preferred the term "deaconesses." In most Baptist history,
women in the diaconate have been called deaconesses and have
had a role inferior to that of men in the diaconate. The contemporary trend is for these women to be called deacons, to be ordained,
and to possess all the privileges and duties of male deacons.

A much higher percentage of American Baptist churches have
women in deacon work than do Southern Baptist churches. Norman
H. Maring, church historian at Eastern Baptist Theological Seminary, suggested two possible reasons. To begin with, although the
ordination of deacons is common in the South, it is not so common
in the North. Since ordination is frequently a barrier to women

becoming a part of the diaconate, American Baptist churches which do not ordain deacons are likely more open to women in the diaconate. Also, while deacons in the South generally continue to be the most important group of officers in the church, trustees are often the most important officers and possess the most authority in churches in the North. Contrary to the past, deacons usually do not have the same status in American Baptist churches as they do in Southern Baptist churches. This makes it easier for women to become deacons in the former.[50]

Conclusion

Baptist churches in the 1800s considered deacons to be vital to their life. The churches entrusted numerous and significant responsibilities in the hands of deacons and had an obvious respect for them. Deacons found themselves functioning more and more in the realm of church business as the "board" concept developed and grew. This narrowing of the scope of deacon work prompted responses from several Baptist leaders who appealed for a fuller involvement of deacons in the spiritual ministries of churches. These leaders pointed to the New Testament as the basis for their arguments.

The twentieth century opened with actual practices in churches still leaning heavily in the direction of administrative work for deacons. Simultaneously, the call for diaconal investment in pastoral ministries began to mount. Deacons were urged not to confine their labor too closely to church business and not to misuse their authority, but to become spiritual leaders of their congregations and models of servanthood. As a result, many churches implemented a broader vision of ministry for their deacons.

Since 1950 Southern Baptists have created particularly valuable resources and programs for deacons which have strongly emphasized the need for deacons to understand and activate the concept of servanthood designated for them in the New Testament. Thousands of churches have profited by implementing the Deacon Family Ministry Plan and by using *The Deacon* and other materials to help their deacons minister more effectively.

Like the latter 1700s, the past several years have been a time when women have been more prominent in the diaconate than usual. Basic thrusts toward liberty and liberation in American life in the 1770s and the 1970s lay behind and within both these periods and aided the cause of women. Women deacons flourish best in a time such as the present, when the diaconate is interpreted more in terms of a wide range of supporting and caring ministries than more narrowly in terms of church management and business administration.

4

LESSONS FROM DEACON HISTORY

Although many lessons emerge from a study of deacon history, four seem particularly important: the necessity for deacons to serve, the possibility for them to lose their effectiveness, the urgency for them to lead, and the challenge for them to support and minister to their pastor. These lessons may appear rather obvious, but perhaps a realistic assessment of them can contribute positively to the direction of contemporary deacon trends.

Lesson 1

Deacons exist to serve God and the church.—Service is integral to the New Testament name for a deacon *(diakonos* or servant). Service lies behind the biblical qualifications for deacons in 1 Timothy 3. Although the New Testament says little about the precise duties of deacons, churches of the early centuries assigned a variety of servant roles to them. These churches interpreted the New Testament to mean that deacons were to minister.

The earliest Baptists read the New Testament the same way. John Smyth, pastor of the first Baptist congregation, stated in 1609 that deacons should be ordained so they could serve church members in this special capacity. This pattern of thinking continued through Baptist history with similar, though sometimes less fervent, degrees of emphasis. The current Deacon Family Ministry Plan of Southern Baptists accents to a high level the need for deacons to view their primary function as that of caring ministry.

In the Middle Ages the office of deacon was a preliminary stage of training enabling a person to advance the clerical ladder and become a full-fledged minister or priest. The good news of the Bible contradicts this low concept of the deaconship and affirms that the office of deacon is a full ministry in its own right. The New Testament does not divide into grades of importance those Christians who serve God and the church. Not only does Scripture place deacons in a work of service; it also treats them as exemplary models of servanthood for all other church members.

What is required if deacons are to serve effectively? A careful understanding of biblical qualifications, of historical precedents, and of practical possibilities can help. A rearrangement of priorities in deacon work may be in order. A new view of deacons as ministers in a service, instead of officers in a position, might be the answer. Other factors could be more adequate attention to the deacon selection process, to deacon orientation and ordination, to continuing training opportunities for deacons, and to the cultivation of personal spiritual discipline by deacons.

The potential areas of deacon service are unlimited. Deacons can engage in such diverse ministries as teaching, preaching, visiting, becoming involved in social action, counseling, leading in charitable giving, organizing, administrating, carrying out the Lord's Supper, and meeting basic needs of the pastor. Deacon history has demonstrated the need for flexibility in what deacons do in individual churches. Forms of deacon ministry are endless—depending, of course, on the creative imagination of each local church and the deacons in it.

All this is not to suggest that deacons who devote their full time to implementing a broad range of spiritual services should become paid staff members of a church. Deacons are not paid, and the continuation of this pattern will work to the advantage of churches and deacons. The strength of deacon ministries lies heavily in the voluntary nature of their labor. Laypeople identify best with this kind of servant model, which is based on a solid understanding of the doctrine of the priesthood of believers. Churches do well when they view their deacons as leaders and facilitators in ministry, not as church officials who, along with professional staff members, do all church ministry in behalf of other church members.

If deacon bodies are to minister well, at least six needs are imperative. First, deacons will share opportunities for service among themselves. Too much demand will render an individual deacon's work ineffective; proper division of assignments will enhance the accomplishments of each deacon. Second, they are able to affirm that their primary reason for being is to involve themselves in ministries of compassion and helpfulness. Third, they need specific preparation for each kind of ministry to which they commit themselves. Fourth, they will try to keep informed of the latest trends and resources regarding deacon ministries. The best way to do this is to subscribe to *The Deacon,* a publication of the Sunday School Board of the Southern Baptist Convention. Fifth, they will cooperate with the church staff to assure them that the church is pursuing a common mission. Sixth, they will stay close to God and the Bible in their morality and spirituality.

Deacons are ideally a people of vision, excitement, and creative energy. These characteristics can give to every deacon ministry a new level of appeal and significance.

To translate this into concrete illustration, consider the role of deacons in the Lord's Supper. This ordinance can be much more than a perfunctory routine of simply passing around the bread and the cups. Innovative deacons can prepare for and experience the supper in several valuable ways. They can share in a retreat focusing on the meaning of the supper and their role in it. They can alert church members by telephone of the date for the next celebration of the ordinance and urge them to read in advance the key biblical passages on the supper and to pray that the supper will lead to new purpose and Christian commitment in their lives. Further, at the end of the ordinance deacons can distribute among themselves and interested church members cards describing specific ministries needing to be done by those receiving the cards.

Such an approach emphasizes that the sacrifice of Christ symbolized in the supper results in direct and positive service by the church.[1] A number of other stimulating approaches can give freshness and the thrill of ministry to the supper or to any other service requiring attention by deacons.

Lesson 2

A wise church will guard carefully against the possibility of deacon decline.—History has amply proven that many factors can lead to a decline in the role of deacons as church servants. Some of these factors merit description because of the ways they have retarded deacon progress in the past.

To restrict deacon roles too narrowly can harm deacon effectiveness. This happened in the Eastern Church in the Middle Ages when the liturgical (worship) tasks of deacons became so predominant that their primary role as agents of charity and practical ministries lessened considerably. According to some, the deacons in certain contemporary Baptist churches have fallen into the same kind of trap. Through excessive attention focused on deacon involvement in the Lord's Supper and in church business management, as important as both areas may be, other equally significant areas of ministry sometimes are neglected. Churches where this pattern exists may want to provide and insist on more diversified ministries for their deacons. The participation of deacons in a responsible approach to the Deacon Family Ministry Plan can be significant in alleviating this problem.

To let the concepts of office, position, or status take priority over servant functions can be detrimental to the deacon role. Deacon life in the Western Church in the Middle Ages dwindled in importance when the function of deacon ministry became subordinated to the privileges and prestige of the office. Perhaps the best counterbalance to this potential source of decline is to reread the biblical accounts which surround deacons with servant ideals.

To allow deacons to exceed the bounds of their authority can neutralize their effectiveness and tarnish their image. Church records stated at the outset of Baptist life in seventeenth-century England that deacons who assumed illegitimate power were to be disciplined. The thrust of the Baptist heritage is that deacons are to serve and lead—not to rule and govern. Proper provisions in the church constitution, more adequate views of deacon ordination, and an emphasis on deacon accountability to the church can prevent this problem.

To place too many responsibilities on deacons can lead to frustration and inefficient ministry on their part. Deacons are church leaders who deserve respect. They are not respected when fellow church members dump in their laps all the work they know needs to be done but are unwilling to do themselves. This evasion of responsibility deprives the membership at large of vital opportunities in ministry, and it creates a functional overload for deacons. This problem understandably robs deacons of their spiritual energies and stifles their initiative. Shared ministry with deacons at the forefront seems preferable.

For deacons to adopt programs of ministry which they neglect to fulfill can lead to disillusionment for them and the congregation. The Deacon Family Ministry Plan is a prime example. When deacons announce their intention to begin this excellent approach to family ministry, some important things happen both to the deacons and to the families in the church. While the deacons place upon themselves a major duty to families, the families develop the feeling that they are now going to be ministered to in a special way. If the families receive such ministry, the whole church prospers. If, however, deacons fail to do their intended ministries to families, deacons suffer from inconsistency; and church families hurt because of unmet needs and dissatisfaction with their leadership. Perhaps a good guideline for preventing such a problem is for deacon bodies to honestly evaluate their intentions and communicate realistic expectations to the congregation before entering major ministry projects. Deacon decline is possible where these or similar problems exist. Preventive discipline is essential. A meaningful devotional life adds positive nurture to the spiritual development of a deacon. Close attachment to a deacon's primary goal—Christian service—can add daily maturity. Other points likely to assure integrity and a forward thrust for deacons include emphases on their biblical foundations and on the desperate need which churches have for their ministries. With the superior resources available today to help deacons do their work well, their future in Baptist life should be marked by a continuing surge of growth and maturity.

Lesson 3

Churches look to their deacons for leadership.—Churches authorize the election of deacons, confirm their work in ordination, and give them many of the most important tasks in church life. Such election, ordination, and assignments in ministry place deacons in prominent and clearly visible roles. Churches expect their deacons to be models in ministry, to exhibit exemplary life-styles, and to offer guidance and direction for many aspects of a church's mission.

Three things happen once deacons are ordained. For one thing, they find that their lives are placed under constant scrutiny by the rest of the congregation. This does not imply that the church is looking for character flaws to be exposed. Rather, it means that church members are earnestly searching for wise counsel and strong leadership. The church wants its deacons to reflect Christ.

Also, deacons now discover that they have a special platform from which they can be spiritual motivators and facilitators. They realize that they, too, can help "to equip God's people for work in his service" (Eph. 4:12, NEB). The cumulative impact of the Baptist past suggests that in ordination deacons become enablers in caring for the needs of church families and individuals and in leading these people to care for others. Deacons are "table ministers" of the Lord, the pastor, the poor, and others. Their excitement about Christian ministry radiates magnetically to all church members who will receive it and in turn offer it to others.

A further result of ordination for deacons is their recognition that their new leadership role entails responsibility in their personal lives. They are to provide a strong example in financial stewardship, to participate fully in the Bible study and worship opportunities of the church, to present a powerful witness to Christ in daily living, and in more ways to show that Christ is Lord. The nature of deacons' abilities to lead others depends largely on their skills in disciplining their own lives. Soundness in character will help a deacon make the best use of leadership privileges.

Deacons do well to distinguish between leadership and domination. Leadership occurs when they seek the best for the church under the guidance of God. Domination exists when they abandon the direction of God and seek to rule from the perspective of personal advantage. An easy way for deacons to become dominators is to identify so closely with church business matters that they relegate to an inferior status their biblical roles of servanthood in other equally important ministries. Genuine leadership becomes a reality as deacons lose all desire for selfish gain through a wholesome investment of their lives in meeting a broad range of spiritual needs.

The presence of deacons throughout Baptist history, coupled with the intensified encouragement being given to them today in written resources and conferences and by other means, shows that Baptists continue to recognize the value of their leadership in churches. Is it possible that deacons, since there are so many more of them than pastors, have the best potential of all Baptist leaders to shape the patterns of mission and ministry in local churches? If deacons under the lordship of Christ will seriously implement their leadership possibilities, the progress of Baptist life is without limitation.

Why give so much attention to the leadership role of deacons when there are also other kinds of leaders in churches? Two reasons seem appropriate. One is that the quality of a congregation's life seldom exceeds that of its deacons. The more basic reason is that the New Testament singles out deacons as special servants. Without including specific duties for deacons, the qualifications for them in First Timothy 3 imply that they must have had major leadership roles in ministry. Deacon history reveals that Baptists have interpreted the New Testament to mean just this. Deacons are leaders by biblical and historical precedents, and contemporary Baptists do well to honor their deacons and respect their leadership.

Lesson 4

Compassionate deacons minister to their pastor.—One theme which has stretched itself through the history of Baptist deacons as much as any other is that deacons are table servants. This theme is biblical since the original meaning of *diakonos* (servant or deacon) was apparently a table waiter who walked barefoot through dust to serve dining guests. Baptists have usually spoken of three kinds of tables requiring the attention of deacons—those of the Lord, the poor, and the minister. Most recognize the involvement of deacons in the Lord's Supper, and this book has pointed to the need for deacons to care for the poor, as well as others in distress. But what about the table of the minister?

A pastor has many needs—financial, emotional, spiritual, intellectual, and others. The demands on a pastor's time are normally heavy and can occasionally become almost overwhelming. Weddings, funerals, hospital calls, counseling, community visitation, sermon preparation, administration, and other important tasks require enormous outlays of energy. Unless the pastor receives support and relief, the pressures of ministry can lead to frustration.

Since 1 Timothy 3 ties bishops and deacons so closely together, deacons have biblical encouragement to form a colleagueship with their pastor in which mutual support becomes fundamental. Working in relationship to assure steady leadership for the church, the two cultivate a sensitivity toward assisting one another in every way possible.

Deacons can aid their pastor immensely by staying in touch with his needs. This awareness can then result in specific action. Deacons can first urge the congregation to do certain things for the pastor: to provide adequate compensation for him, including salary, housing, car allowance, annuity, and other benefits; to free him of a never-ending flow of activity so that he can have deserved time with his family in recreation, with his God in personal devotion, and with his books in study; and to help him stay mentally stimulated by providing conference and convention time, buying materials for his library, and offering him opportunities in continuing theological education.

Besides leading the congregation to support the pastor, deacons can give direct support of their own. They can assist him best by constant and careful attention to their responsibilities. This will involve absorbing pastoral involvements, especially in the area of family ministry. Deacons can create a climate of acceptance and genuine care so that the pastor will be able to discuss with them his deep feelings about his ministry and life. Deacons do well to build up their pastor by engaging only in constructive conversation about him and defending him against unjust criticism.

In the event of a pastor's sickness or any similar crisis, deacons can be particularly valuable partners in ministry. While I. V. Couch, pastor of the Millers Creek Baptist Church in Millers Creek, North Carolina, was hospitalized in 1978 for twenty-three days because of major surgery, five deaths occurred in his church family. After returning home, Couch strongly commended his deacons: "Thanks to the Deacon Family Ministry Plan, they helped by making the initial visit to the home, alerting those responsible for meals (all funerals were out of town), seeing that the church was represented at the services and making follow-up visits to the homes of the bereaved. The strain and stress upon their pastor was much less because he had the assurance that the deacons were caring for those families." [2]

Deacons will do well to offer consideration and ministry to the pastor's family, too. The pastor's wife and children have a unique relationship to the church. Because they live under high expectations and are so often on the giving end of ministry, their own emotional and spiritual needs can easily be neglected by a congregation. Deacons can help prevent such neglect through conscientious concern and compassion. Deacons who agree to support their pastor and his family in every way possible will find new meaning in their church membership and in their ordained position.

Conclusion

Valuable lessons evolve from deacon history. These lessons point deacons to the New Testament and direct them toward increased quality in ministry and leadership. Fully understood, such lessons can be a channel of creative vision and service. Fully implemented, they can be a source of remarkable achievement. When deacons serve and lead in imitation of Christ, a church can make substantial progress in fulfilling its call to God's purposes.

The fundamental impact of the past is that in deacons God has special church servants through whom he continues to share a ministry of compassion.

5

A KEY ISSUE FACING DEACONS

Many important issues confront contemporary Baptist deacons. How will they respond to the accelerating thrust toward increased involvement by them in the pastoral ministries of the church? How will deacon groups relate to the growing number of women in the diaconate? Will deacons seek training opportunities and take advantage of the resources available to help them do their work more effectively? These and other issues are surfacing and receiving significant discussion in deacon life today.

But the key issue is whether deacons are measuring up to the challenging qualifications provided for them in 1 Timothy 3:8-13. The urgent need for deacons to live holy and righteous lives lies realistically at the foundation of their biblical identity and their ministry. Any failure to consider this issue would make meaningless the discussion of other issues concerning deacons. First Timothy gives no definition of deacon duties, only qualifications. Perhaps the biblical point is that character must precede function.

Frank Stagg wrote that "The standards *demanded* of bishops and deacons [in 1 Timothy 3] are high, but they are no higher than those *expected* of all Christians." [1] This claim rightfully places all Christians under common biblical requirements. Two points emerge, however. First, although the qualifications may apply to all Christians, the passage isolates deacons and directs the qualifications specifically to them. Second, this emphasis implies that deacons in their roles of service and leadership are to exemplify the qualifications in a particularly effective way. As A. T. Robertson put it, although every church member has the same general Christian duties as church officers, "the preacher and deacon cannot escape an extra responsibility because of their leadership." [2]

In his letter to Timothy, Paul describes deacon standards as follows: "Deacons likewise must be serious, not double-tongued, not addicted to much wine, not greedy for gain; they must hold the mystery of the faith with a clear conscience. And let them also be tested first; then if they prove themselves blameless let them serve as deacons. The women likewise must be serious, no slanderers, but temperate, faithful in all things. Let deacons be the husband of one wife, and let them manage their children and their households well; for those who serve well as deacons gain a good standing for themselves and also great confidence in the faith which is in Christ Jesus" (1 Tim. 3:8-13). What do these qualifications mean?

Verse 8 telescopes four qualifications into a few words. The word "serious" suggests that deacons are not to be frivolous in performing their tasks but are to be church leaders of dignity, respect, and high principles. This does not mean that they are to stifle their enjoyment of life. Rather, they are to live life to the fullest understanding that in a special sense they are representatives of Christ and his claims on the church.

Deacons are not to be "double-tongued." They are to be honest in their conversations and are not to engage in double-talk or insincerity. One implication is that deacons are not to say one thing and mean another. Another is that they are not to misrepresent their thoughts or feelings on a topic by expressing them to different people in opposing ways. This spiritual standard has obvious relevance for Baptist deacons who circulate from home to home in their ministry to families.

Next, deacons should be church leaders who are "not addicted to much wine." They are not to harm their personal lives and reputations, to provide an unhealthy influence on others, or to make a mockery of their ministry by yielding to an urge to use anything over which they may eventually have no mastery in their lives. Deacons cannot function well for Christ and the church if they occasionally or regularly lose control of their rational faculties, their personal appearance, their sense of self-esteem, or their concern for the welfare of others. Excessive drinking has led to alcoholism for millions of Americans, resulting in destroyed lives, wrecked marriages, children in emotional turmoil, lost work hours, deaths on highways, and other major problems. My mother died from a car accident caused by an intoxicated driver. Christ calls deacons to a constructive life-style and gives them command over all human passions which otherwise can lead to ultimate ruin.

The fourth ideal for deacons is that they not be "greedy for gain." Such greed can lead a person to disreputable ways of getting money. This qualification applies both to the personal and business life of deacons and to their role in the church. Deacons could be tempted to direct the use of church funds toward their own particular interests. The intent of this ideal is that deacons, rather than be greedy, should express through their ministry the self-giving, compassionate pattern of Christ.

When the executive committee of the Laymen's Missionary Movement made its annual report to the Southern Baptist Convention in 1925, it stated that during the preceding year its members had given much attention to the biblical qualifications for deacons. The committee then related these qualifications to the stewardship of money. Quite the opposite of being "greedy for gain," every deacon, according to the committee report, should be "willing to obey the scriptural requirement to bring his tithe and offering into the Lord's storehouse upon the first day of every week" and "should appreciate the significance of his example in this matter." [3] This advice deserves contemporary application, too.

Verse 9 establishes for deacons an important association between faith and practice. Deacons "must hold the mystery of the faith with a clear conscience." The "mystery" refers to the eternal truth of God which was hidden until made known by divine revelation in Jesus Christ. Deacons can be true leaders in the Christian faith only if their allegiance to God's revelation in Christ is so complete that they can claim purity of conscience. The goal for deacons is to achieve consistency between holding to Christ and living for him. Responsible deacons know and share the purpose of God in Christ, and their lives reflect moral and spiritual integrity. In an age when credibility gaps afflict leaders in many phases of political, social, and religious life, Baptist deacons are in a unique position to be standard-bearers to the truth of God for his people.

Verse 10 recommends that persons be tested and proven blameless before serving in the diaconal role. Baptist churches have interpreted this variously to mean either an actual trial period when a candidate for deacon was placed under close scrutiny or, more generally, the basic evaluation of the church on the previous lifestyle of the candidate. The heart of the matter is that churches are to be extremely careful about who they place in the diaconate. Not every person on the membership role of a church is worthy to be a deacon. Deacons must be members who have already demonstrated faithfulness to God and the church and who are willing to pledge themselves to continued commitment.

Verse 11 lists qualifications for "the women" which briefly indicate demands comparable to those placed on the deacons. Whether these women are wives of deacons or women deacons, the qualifications are valid since either group would need them. The call to be "serious" has the same meaning here as it does for deacons in verse 8. That the women not be "slanderers" is similar to the claim that deacons not be "double-tongued." The women are not to gossip, to make false accusations, or to defame the character of others. Last, they are to be temperate and reliable.

The literal translation of verse 12 is "Let deacons be the husband of one wife." The complexity of the background situation and the ambiguity of the grammar make it difficult to know whether the writer was concerned about the single life, polygamy, divorce, remarriage after divorce, or remarriage after the death of a wife. Although the writer could have meant one or more of these possibilities, this qualification for deacons must be read in light of the wholesome commitment to marriage and the family which permeates Scripture. Polygamy is certainly an anti-Christian practice which violates the biblical ideal of two—not three or more—becoming one in marriage. On the other hand, singleness and remarriage after the natural death of one's wife are practices which are generally approved in the Bible.

The issue of ordaining deacons who have been divorced must be dealt with in the light of what Jesus and Paul said about divorce and remarriage after divorce. The ideal underlying all New Testament teachings on marriage is that this covenant between a man and a woman is designed by God to be permanent.

Because of the massive dimensions of the divorce problem in America, churches will do well to establish a high marital standard as a criterion for selecting their deacons. This is not to deny acceptance of the divorced by God and the church, to forget the value of the divorced before God, or to rule out the possibility that certain divorced people can make excellent church leaders. Rather, any condoning of widespread divorce among church leadership could easily jeopardize the biblical foundation of marriage and family life. In this age of fractured families, Baptist deacons can help churches by reflecting the biblical model in their marriages.

Another qualification for deacons in verse 12 is that they should "manage their children and their households well." This highlights again the need for deacons to cultivate quality family relationships. When deacons are good leaders of their homes, they provide an excellent example for others in their churches. Because deacons are leaders in their churches, those who show good leadership skills in their homes are likely to be of more value to their churches.

Verse 13 concludes the section on deacons in 1 Timothy 3 with the promise that "deacons with a good record of service may claim a high standing and the right to speak openly on matters of the Christian faith" (NEB). Deacons who minister effectively gain respect from fellow Christians and a position of trust and influence

in the church. Effective ministry also builds boldness in service
and witness and an increased awareness that a deacon is doing
the will of God. These promises are incentives for deacons to meet
all the qualifications laid out for them.

What can deacons do if they find, after studying the biblical
standards, that they are not meeting one or more of the qualifications? What can they do if they realize that they are not living
out the servant theme so vital to the biblical nature of the diaconate?
First, they can confess to God and other deacons their failure to
deal responsibly with the high calling given them by the church
in ordination. Second, they can ask God for a fresh vision of their
task and the courage to meet its demands.

Are the qualifications in 1 Timothy 3:8-13 the only biblical standards expected of deacons? Obviously not. Deacons are as responsible to heed the Ten Commandments, the Sermon on the Mount,
and the rest of Scripture as are all Christians. That deacons receive
special attention in 1 Timothy says, however, that they are unique
servants of God and the church. Both the electing congregation
and the serving deacons need to give careful consideration to the
moral and spiritual credentials of deacons.

Deacons can minister to families more effectively by living lives
that express an uncompromising attachment to basic biblical principles. This immovable allegiance to New Testament qualifications
will cultivate character development in the congregation at large
and will provide an avenue for meeting the needs of church families
who admire the high moral qualities and spiritual zeal of their
deacons.

A 1937 writing pinpointed a kind of ministry for Baptist deacons
which bears repeating: "there is an unlimited amount of shepherding to be done, which cannot possibly be done properly except
under the guidance of . . . deacons."[4] In order for deacons to
assume the urgent shepherding role in today's society, they need
credentials worthy of imitation by those to whom they minister.
These credentials include, among other things, a strong character,

a pure conscience, and a willingness to share testimony of the unchallenged place of Christ in their lives. The Bible pleads for this kind of deacon.'

Conclusion

Because the servant concept saturates every biblical thought about deacons, certain qualities are specified for them. The clear implication is that deacon ministry and qualifications cannot be separated. One without the other is functionally impractical. Deacons who try to minister without adequate credentials weaken their influence. Those who claim the qualifications but fail to minister have little substance to their calling. Those, however, who combine biblical qualifications with opportunities for ministry into positive relationships are living out the purpose of their ordination.

6

DEACONS IN COVENANT

The editor of *The Deacon* recently wrote, "Deacons in an increasing number of churches across the Southern Baptist Convention are writing their own deacon covenants." [1] This significant trend shows that deacons are willing to live disciplined lives and to take seriously the ministries available to them.

A deacon covenant is a series of pledges which deacons voluntarily make to God, the church, the pastor, and one another. The covenant reflects biblical guidelines by which the deacons intend to conduct themselves or practice their Christian faith. A commitment to meet the moral and spiritual obligations of the office of deacon is central to covenantal vows.

Covenants are a valid and valuable part of Baptist life. They have a strong basis in the Bible, theology, history, and proven practice. The church renewal movement in modern American Christianity has plainly demonstrated the practical advantages of covenants in churches. Deacons willing to covenant themselves before their congregation to a high level of Christian ethics and spirituality will experience personal renewal and make a vital contribution to their church. Healthy use of a covenant implies continuing renewal of commitments. Serving as a constant reminder of responsibilities, a covenant points deacons toward the integrity that ought to be theirs. Through the stress on a disciplined life-style, the promises made by deacons cultivate an excitement and an innovative spirit for their ministry. Also, a covenant can promote regular evaluation of the maturity and achievements of deacons.

Other values can come from a deacon covenant. Since such an agreement consists of biblical disciplines which deacons are expected to observe, it gives them an opportunity to define and emphasize those disciplines. The act of struggling with, thinking through, and writing down the disciplines helps deacons come to terms with basic Christian standards for guiding their lives.

Deacons can deepen the quality of their fellowship through a covenant. As they voluntarily commit themselves to God, the church, the pastor, and one another, they will gain a fresh sense of Christian caring and community. This will be an enormously helpful incentive for increased investment of themselves in family ministries. In a collective pledge to common biblical tasks, deacons mold themselves together to meet the objectives of the church.

A deacon covenant carefully prepared and effectively implemented can be a model stimulating the entire church to write and adopt a covenant. Church members who see their deacons conscientiously carry out their duties may well be motivated to give more attention to the quality of their own churchmanship. This is an age when "ethical compromises, spiritual convenience, church attendance with minimal involvement, an occasional nod to God, the spectator syndrome, and the view of God and the church as optional are characteristic of a fairly common approach to church membership." [2] In such a time deacons who activate God's will for themselves in a covenantal bond can give impetus to a covenantal awakening in the larger congregation. In raising a church's consciousness of what it means to have a regenerate membership, deacons can perform one of their finest ministries.

Guidelines for Writing a Covenant

Deacons in each church will receive maximum benefit by preparing their own covenant. Examination of covenants written by deacons in other churches can be helpful, but simply to adopt a covenant developed by another deacon body may negate the positive values that emerge from personal and creative encounter with the disciplines which are vital to covenantal preparation. Deacons who prepare their own covenant can design it to give priority to those biblical teachings which need special consideration at that juncture in their common life. Also, such a covenant will be a more meaningful and functional document since it will reflect the intentions and meet the individual needs of the deacons who draw it up and approve it. Several steps are required to make a covenant a reality.[3]

1. *Create interest in a deacon covenant by showing its possible values.*— The pastor can do this through a series of devotionals in consecutive deacons' meetings or in a special focus on covenants in a deacons' retreat. In either setting he could examine the biblical, theological, historical, and practical dimensions of the covenant idea. Also, the deacon chairman or any other deacon or group of deacons can take the initiative to bring this concept to the attention of all deacons. When the values of covenanting are clear, deacons will be more willing to look closely at the quality of their commitments and to state them in written form.

2. *Select a deacon covenant committee.*—Neither the pastor nor any one deacon or group of deacons can presume to write a covenant for an entire deacon group. Such a covenant would have minimal authority and even less appeal for the deacons at large. A more workable approach is for the deacons in business session, upon a formal recommendation, to appoint a covenant committee who will coordinate the designing of the covenant. This committee will be responsible to the whole deacon body at every point in its work. All committee members need to possess the highest possible moral and spiritual credentials, since they will be drafting a document intended to nurture integrity in deacon life.

3. *Adopt principles for deciding the contents of the covenant.*—A good starting place is to affirm that every element in the covenant will have a biblical basis. A deacon covenant does not replace the Bible; it summarizes biblical duties and calls for their application. Alongside this, the committee will find it helpful to form the covenant around biblical principles for guiding conduct rather than around

rules for governing the practice of faith. To give the words in a covenant a legalistic meaning is a mistake; to focus on the biblical intention behind the words is a more appropriate emphasis.

Next, the committee will need to decide whether to stress specific or general responsibilities in the covenant. If it is overly specific, it can become legal, long, and narrow in scope and application. If it is too general, it can become vague and of little value. Perhaps the following guideline can help: "A covenant ought to be specific enough to state concrete commitments, disciplines, and expectations, but it should be general enough to allow for flexibility in interpretation." [4] This will make clear the position of deacons on matters of Christian conduct and give full allowance for the priesthood of believers.

One other principle to consider is whether to phrase the covenant in terms of positive features of Christian conduct to imitate or negative features of non-Christian conduct to avoid. Whereas a deacon covenant characterized by the negative approach offers little affirmative guidance, one created with a positive thrust accents biblical ethics more adequately and calls deacons to a healthy lifestyle and ministry.

4. *Define the contents.*—Stay close to the Bible in determining the contents. State clearly at the outset that the covenant is primarily a pledge to God and then a series of vows to the church, the pastor, and other deacons. This approach will place the covenant in its proper theological context. A deacon covenant makes sense only as a response of gratitude to the prior covenantal initiative of God through Jesus Christ.

The contents need to be comprehensive in scope as they identify principles for conduct in all basic areas of deacon life. The excellent deacon covenant of the First Baptist Church of Shreveport, Louisiana, illustrates well how to achieve this.[5] The preamble expresses a commitment to the teachings and spirit of 1 Timothy 3:8-13. The first section then focuses on the life of the deacon and presents pledges related to personal life, vocation, home, and church. The last section centers on the work of the deacon and describes commitments relating to witness, worship, pastoral ministries, and active participation in the deacon body itself. A covenantal bond with the pastor is implied throughout. As a minimum, any deacon covenant can appeal for deacons to pray, to study the Bible, to attend church and deacons' meetings, to engage in ministry, and to express strong stewardship of money.

5. *Secure the input and approval of other deacons.*—Write the first draft. This will be a preliminary effort of the covenant committee to assimilate and state their basic thoughts. After approval by the committee, reproduce a copy of the draft for all deacons. Also, give them a list of the principles used in developing the draft. Urge them to study the proposal carefully and to write down suggested changes and give them to the committee. The committee will then prepare a second draft, incorporating the strengths of the suggestions. This draft can also be shared with all deacons and then further altered, if necessary. The committee then writes the final draft for presentation to the deacon body in business session. The purpose of this approach is to make sure that the covenant belongs to all the deacons, not simply to a committee of deacons.

6. *Print and distribute the covenant.*—After a deacon group approves a covenant, they will want to have it printed for distribution to all present and future deacons. The printing of a covenant does not mean that it can never be changed. A progressive concept needs to underlie the making of the covenant. Fresh insight from the Holy Spirit, new understanding of biblical teachings, and the rise of new needs and emphases within a deacon body are only a few of the factors which may require periodic change in a covenant.

Suggestions for Using a Covenant

A deacon covenant assumes its truest meaning when viewed primarily as a relationship rather than a document. Any use to which a written covenant can be put that will make it a functional tool for growth in the relationship of deacons to God, the church, the pastor, and one another will be a good use.

Deacons in several churches are already implementing their covenants in significant ways. The Beechmont Baptist Church in Louisville, Kentucky, is a good example.[6] The deacons here give real strength to their covenant by voluntarily signing it before the congregation at the time of their ordination. This practice has three major advantages. It confronts deacons with their covenant obligations at the front end of their office and ministry. The penning of their names on the dotted line of commitment reenforces in the minds of the deacons the need to meet the biblical standards comprising the covenant. Last, this approach exposes the self-imposed disciplines of the deacons to the full visibility of the congregation and emphasizes further the urgency of fulfilling the responsibilities described in the covenant. The Beechmont Church also gives each new deacon a special copy of the covenant signed by the pastor and chairman of deacons. Further, once a year an opportunity is given for all deacons to face again their original commitments.

A deacon body will certainly want to alert candidates for the diaconate to the covenant prior to their ordination so that they can see in advance the obligations they will be assuming. Present deacons will do well not to place covenantal demands on new deacons that they are unwilling to undertake for themselves. To do so would create an illegitimate double standard of commitment which might nullify much of a covenant's potential usefulness. A covenant which functions well applies to all who agree to its contents.

Deacons can give special attention to their covenant in selected meetings or in retreats. This can be appropriately done in the deacons' meeting preceding the celebration of the Lord's Supper in the church. This can prepare deacons for meaningful participation in the ordinance, which has a strong covenantal motif (1 Cor. 11:25). A number of valuable things can be done to focus on covenantal pledges. The covenant can be read responsively or in unison. Sections of it can be studied in detail with particular stress on the biblical background of each section. The covenantal meaning of the Lord's Supper can be examined closely. Renewal of covenantal commitments can be made. Through extended periods of prayer, the Holy Spirit can be approached for guidance on how to make the contents of the covenant a reality in daily life. ·

An annual Deacon Covenant Day can be an effective way to enhance covenantal allegiance. On this day all deacons can reaffirm before the congregation their vows to God, the church, the pastor, and one another. This emphasis tells a church that its deacons are honestly trying to implement the duties and qualities required of them in the New Testament. Also, it heightens the congregation's awareness of their covenantal responsibilities.

Perhaps the best approach to covenant practices for deacons is one that is comprehensive and consistent. Principles in a covenant need to apply to a deacon's whole life and to command the attention of all deacons. A covenant will become a useful tool for moral and spiritual maturation as deacons cultivate consistency between the pledges they make and the lives they live. Successful completion of the duties of deaconship is essential to the well-being of a church; and these duties cannot be postponed, ignored, or treated casually. An approach to a covenant which gives high priority to the obligations described in it can assist deacons to meet the challenges of their ministry. Deacons in each church will need to implement their covenant in their own unique ways.

Conclusion

Deacons live in relationships. They talk with God. They minister to their church. They support their pastor. They share with one another. They function best when wholesomely committed to all their partners in Christian service. This commitment takes concrete form when written into a deacon covenant. Such an agreement solidifies deacons around common guidelines for practicing their faith in the totality of their relationships.

Each deacon body is urged to consider preparing its own covenant. This collective involvement in pinpointing and developing loyalty to basic biblical principles for conduct and ministry can lead to a resurgence in deacon character and compassion. As deacons come alive for Christ, their entire church will receive new incentive to open the Bible with fresh vision, to pray with more intensity, to worship with more vitality, to contribute with more generosity, and to serve God with more consecration.

This chapter on deacon covenants could easily be subtitled "A Disciplined Move into the Future." While this book has focused mainly on the history of deacons, the purpose has been to provide perspective enabling contemporary deacons to surge into tomorrow with a better understanding of their role. Solid devotion to the biblical disciplines placed in a deacon covenant can assist this forward thrust.

Notes

CHAPTER 1

1. C. E. B. Cranfield, "Diakonia in the New Testament," *Service in Christ,* ed. James I. McCord and T. H. L. Parker (Grand Rapids: William B. Eerdmans, 1966), p. 45.

2. Cyprian, *Epistles,* X.1 in *The Ante-Nicene Fathers* (cited hereafter as *ANF*), 5:291; Eusebius, *Church History,* VII.ii.24 in *The Nicene and Post-Nicene Fathers* (cited hereafter as *NPNF*), 2d series, 1:301; *Apostolic Constitutions,* II.iii.xvi in *ANF,* 7:402; Hermas, *Similitudes,* IX.xxvi in *ANF,* 2:52; R. Hugh Connolly, ed., *Didascalia Apostolorum* (Oxford: Clarendon Press, 1929), p. 150; Eusebius, *Church History,* VII.xxi.7-8 in *NPNF,* 2d ser., 1:307.

3. Gregory Dix, ed., *The Apostolic Tradition of St. Hippolytus* (London: SPCK, 1968), p. 57; Pseudo-Clement, *Epistle to James,* xii in *ANF,* 8:220; Connolly, p. 148.

4. *Martyrdom of Habib the Deacon* in *ANF,* 8:690-695.

5. Dix, p. 60; Connolly, p. 120; *Apostolic Constitutions,* VIII.ii.xii in *ANF,* 7:486; Ignatius, *Epistle to the Philadelphians,* x in *ANF,* 1:85; Adolf Harnack, *The Mission and Expansion of Christianity in the First Three Centuries,* trans. and ed. James Moffatt (New York: Harper and Brothers, 1961), p. 157.

6. Pseudo-Clement, *Epistle to James,* xii in *ANF,* 8:220.

7. R. P. Symonds, "Deacons in the Early Church," *Theology,* 58, Nov. 1955, p. 409; J. G. Davies, "Deacons, Deaconesses and the Minor Orders in the Patristic Period," *The Journal of Ecclesiastical History,* 14, April 1963, pp. 6-7.

8. Joseph Bingham, *Antiquities of the Christian Church,* vol. 3 (London: William Straker, 1834), p. 225; *Didache,* xv.1-2 in *ANF,* 7:381; Augustine, *Catechising the Uninstructed,* 1.1 in *NPNF,* 1st ser., 3:284.

9. Tertullian, *On Baptism,* xvii in *ANF,* 3:677; Dix, p. 49; Connolly, pp. 146-147; Bingham, pp. 30-31.

10. Justin, *First Apology,* lxv in *ANF,* 1:185; Connolly, p. 117; *Apostolic Constitutions,* II.vii.lvii in *ANF,* 7:421; Dix, pp. 11-12.

11. Dix, p. 15.

12. Ignatius, *Epistle to the Trallians,* vii in *ANF,* 1:69; Connolly, p. 150; Ignatius, *Epistle to the Trallians,* iii in *ANF,* 1:67; Ignatius, *Epistle to the Smyrnaens,* viii in *ANF,* 1:89; *Synod of Antioch in Encaeniis,* canon 4 in *NPNF,* 2d ser., 14:110.

13. Connolly, pp. 146-148.

14. Davies, pp. 3-6.

15. *Apostolic Constitutions,* VIII.iii.xix in *ANF,* 7:492.

16. Lev Gillet, "Deacons in the Orthodox East," *Theology,* 58, Nov. 1955, p. 415; Dix, p. 283.

17. George H. Williams, "The Ministry in the Later Patristic Period (314-451)," *The Ministry in Historical Perspectives,* ed. H. Richard Niebuhr and Daniel D. Williams (New York: Harper & Row, 1956), p. 63.

18. *Apostolic Constitutions,* VIII.iii.xviii in *ANF,* 7:492.

19. J. G. Davies, *The Early Christian Church* (Garden City: Doubleday & Co., 1967), pp. 176-177.

20. Dix, pp. 284-285.

21. Williams, pp. 63-64.

22. Council of Nicaea, canon 18 in *NPNF,* 2d ser., 14:38.

23. D. S. Schaff, "Deaconess," *The New Schaff-Herzog Encyclopedia of Religious Knowledge,* vol. 3 (n.p.: 1909), pp. 374-375.

24. Edward R. Hardy, "Deacons in History and Practice," *The Diaconate Now,* ed. Richard T. Nolan (Washington: Corpus Books, 1968), pp. 23-24.

25. Ibid., pp. 24-25.

26. G. G. Coulton, ed., *A Medieval Garner* (London: Constable & Co., 1910), p. 569.

27. Hardy, p. 26.

28. Schaff, p. 375.

29. Abdel Ross Wentz and Helmut T. Lehmann, eds., *Luther's Works,* vol. 36 (Philadelphia: Muhlenberg Press, 1959), p. 116.

30. John T. McNeill, ed., and Ford Lewis Battles, trans., *Calvin: Institutes of the Christian Religion,* vol. 2, "The Library of Christian Classics, XXI" (London: SCM Press, 1960), p. 1061.

31. Ibid., p. 1062.

32. Guy F. Hershberger, ed., *The Recovery of the Anabaptist Vision* (Scottdale, Pa.: Herald Press, 1957), p. 71; George Huntston Williams and Angel M. Mergal, eds., *Spiritual and Anabaptist Writers,* "The Library of Christian Classics, XXV" (Philadelphia: Westminster Press, 1957), p. 276; William L. Lumpkin, *Baptist Confessions of Faith,* rev. ed. (Valley Forge: Judson Press, 1969), p. 58; H. S. B. Neff, "Deacon," *The Mennonite*

88   The Emerging Role of Deacons

Encyclopedia, vol. 2 (n.p.: 1956), pp. 21-22.

33. Leland H. Carlson, ed., *The Writings of Henry Barrow, 1587-1590,* "Elizabethan Nonconformist Texts, III" (London: George Allen and Unwin, 1962), pp. 219, 609.

34. W. T. Whitley, ed., *The Works of John Smyth,* vol. 1 (Cambridge: University Press, 1915), pp. 260-261.

35. Ibid., p. 261.

36. Ibid., pp. 316-320.

CHAPTER 2

1. W. T. Whitley, ed., *The Works of John Smyth,* vol. 2 (Cambridge: University Press, 1915), pp. 509-510.

2. Thomas Collier, *The Right Constitution and True Subjects of the Visible Church of Christ* (London: Henry Hills, 1654), pp. 30-31.

3. N. Cox, "A Sermon Preached at the Ordination of an Elder and Deacons in a Baptized Congregation in London" (London: Printed for Thomas Fabian, 1681), pp. 12-14.

4. Ibid., p. 15.

5. Elias Keach, *The Glory and Ornament of a True Gospel-Constituted Church* (London: n.p., 1697), p. 11.

6. Edward C. Starr, ed., *A Baptist Bibliography,* vol. 13 (Rochester: American Baptist Historical Society, 1968), p. 29.

7. William L. Lumpkin, *Baptist Confessions of Faith,* rev. ed. (Valley Forge: Judson Press, 1969), p. 101.

8. Ibid., pp. 121-122.

9. Ibid., p. 152.

10. Ibid., p. 166.

11. Ibid., pp. 230-231.

12. W. T. Whitley, ed., *Minutes of the General Assembly of the General Baptist Churches in England with Kindred Records,* vol. 1 (London: Kingsgate Press, n.d.), p. 50.

13. Lumpkin, pp. 122, 231, 287, 319-320.

14. W. T. Whitley, ed., *The Church Books of Ford or Cuddington and Amersham in the County of Bucks* (London: Kingsgate Press, 1912), p. 8.

15. Edward Bean Underhill, ed., *Records of the Churches of Christ Gathered at Fenstanton, Warboys, and Hexham, 1647-1720* (London: Haddon, Brothers, and Co., 1854), pp. 190, 243, 269.

16. Ibid., pp. 243-244.

17. Edward Bean Underhill, ed., *The Records of a Church of Christ Meeting in Broadmead, Bristol, 1640-1687* (London: J. Haddon, 1847), pp. 425-426.

18. Underhill, *Fenstanton, Warboys, and Hexham*, pp. 243-244, 280, 291; Underhill, *Broadmead*, pp. 72, 195, 426, 427.

19. Underhill, *Fenstanton, Warboys, and Hexham*, p. 290; Underhill, *Broadmead*, p. 427.

20. Underhill, *Fenstanton, Warboys, and Hexham*, pp. 18-19; Whitley, *Ford or Cuddington and Amersham*, p. 229.

21. Ibid., pp. 10, 221.

22. Ibid., p. 15.

23. Underhill, *Fenstanton, Warboys, and Hexham*, pp. 16, 18-19.

24. Whitley, *Ford or Cuddington and Amersham*, p. 203.

25. Underhill, *Broadmead*, pp. 72, 195, 396-398, 493-494.

26. William Williams Keen, ed., *The Bicentennial Celebration of the Founding of the First Baptist Church of the City of Philadelphia* (Philadelphia: American Baptist Publication Society, 1889), p. 13.

27. Nathan E. Wood, *The History of the First Baptist Church of Boston* (Philadelphia: American Baptist Publication Society, 1899), p. 368; *Minutes,* First Baptist Church of Boston, September 13, 1685, and August 12, 1688; see *Minutes,* First Baptist Church of Philadelphia, January 16, 1758, for another example of the use of a probationary period; *Minutes,* First Baptist Church of Boston, July 25, 1682.

28. "Minutes from Olde Pennepack Record Books," *The Chronicle,* 1 (July 1938), 126.

29. C. Edwin Barrows, ed., *The Diary of John Comer* (Philadelphia: American Baptist Publication Society, n.d.), pp. 35, 39; *Minutes,* Ashley River Baptist Church, Charleston District, South Carolina, December 12, 1737.

30. Philadelphia Baptist Association, *A Confession of Faith* (Philadelphia: Anderson and Meehan, 1818), pp. 63-64.

31. Ibid., p. 83.

32. *Minutes,* Backus Memorial Baptist Church, North Middleboro, Massachusetts, January 16, 1756; *Minutes,* Welsh Neck Baptist Church, Welsh Neck, South Carolina, September 6, 1760.

33. *Minutes,* Backus Memorial Church, August 14, 1756, and February 5, 1758.

34. *Minutes,* First Baptist Church of Philadelphia, December 20, 1763.

35. *Records of the Welsh Tract Baptist Meeting,* vol. 2 (Wilmington, Del.: Historical Society of Delaware, 1904), p. 8.

36. David Thomas, *The Virginian Baptist* (Baltimore: Enoch Story, 1774), pp. 27-28.

37. James Leo Garrett, Jr., *Baptist Church Discipline* (Nashville: Broadman Press, 1962), p. 34.

38. Morgan Edwards, *The Customs of Primitive Churches* (n.p.: 1774), pp. 36-37.

39. *Minutes*, Warwick Baptist Association, New York, 1796, pp. 7-8.

40. Garrett, p. 34; *Minutes*, Warwick Baptist Association, 1796, pp. 7-8; *Minutes*, Portsmouth Baptist Association, Virginia, 1796, p. 10.

41. E. K. Love, *History of the First African Baptist Church* (Savannah: Morning News Print, 1888), p. 163.

42. Garrett, pp. 40-41.

43. Edwards, *Customs*, p. 37.

44. Ibid., p. 39.

45. Ibid., pp. 40-41.

46. Ibid., p. 43.

47. Morgan Edwards, "Materials Towards a History of the Baptists in the Province of Virginia" (n.p.: 1772), pp. 56-84; G. W. Paschall, "Morgan Edwards' Materials Towards a History of the Baptists in the Province of North Carolina [1772]," *The North Carolina Historical Review*, 7 (July 1930), 384-389; Morgan Edwards, "Materials Towards a History of the Baptists in the Province of South Carolina" (n.p.: 1772), pp. 5, 48; Morgan Edwards, "Materials Towards a History of the Baptists in the Province of Pennsylvania" (n.p.: 1770), p. 67.

48. Paschall, p. 385.

CHAPTER 3

1. William L. Lumpkin, *Baptist Confessions of Faith*, rev. ed. (Valley Forge: Judson Press, 1969), pp. 365-366.

2. Stephen Wright, comp., *History of the Shaftsbury [Vt.] Association from 1781 to 1853* (Troy, N. Y.: A. G. Johnson, 1853), pp. 98-99; Jesse Mercer, *A History of the Georgia Baptist Association* (Washington, Ga.: n.p., 1838), pp. 173-183, 283-288; *Minutes*, Broad River Baptist Association [S. C.], 1830, pp. 6-7; *Minutes*, Salem Baptist Association [Mass.], 1842, pp. 10-14; *Minutes*, Fairfield Baptist Association [Vt.], 1846, p. 10; *Minutes*, New Jersey Baptist Association [N. J.], 1846, p. 19; and *Minutes*, Woodstock Baptist Association [Vt.], 1850, pp. 11-13.

3. B. F. Riley, *A Memorial History of the Baptists in Alabama* (Philadelphia: Judson Press, 1923), p. 28.

4. William Crowell, *The Church Member's Manual* (Boston: Gould, Kendall, and Lincoln, 1845); Edward C. Starr, ed., *A Baptist Bibliography*, vol. 5 (Rochester: American Baptist Publication Society, 1957), p. 197; J. Newton Brown, *The Baptist Church Manual* (Philadelphia: American Baptist Publication Society, 1853); see p. ii of 1957 Judson Press edition of Brown's manual; Edward T. Hiscox, *The Baptist Church Directory* (New York: Sheldon & Co., 1859); Edward T. Hiscox, *The New Directory for Baptist Churches* (Philadelphia: American Baptist Publication Society, 1890), p. 7; J. M. Pendleton, *Church Manual* (Philadelphia: American Baptist Publication Society, 1867); R. Lofton Hudson, "Our Outdated Church Covenant," *Home Missions*, 40 (March 1969), p. 38.

5. Crowell, p. 202.

6. Brown, p. 28; Hiscox, *The Baptist Church Directory*, p. 25.

7. Pendleton, pp. 30-31, 35, 39-40.

8. Theron Brown, *The Canton Baptist Memorial* (Boston: George C. Rand & Avery, 1865), pp. 18, 46, 62; W. T. Hundley, *History of Mattaponi Baptist Church, King and Queen County, Virginia* (Richmond: Appeals Press, n.d.), p. 168; Thomas Armitage, *The Office and Qualifications of a Deacon in the Church* (New York: E. H. Tripp, 1853), pp. 11-20; David Benedict, *Fifty Years Among the Baptists* (New York: Sheldon & Co., 1860), p. 339; J. A. Shackelford, *Deacons: Their Office, Qualifications, and Duties* (Philadelphia: American Baptist Publication Society, 1897), pp. 7, 28-30; R. B. C. Howell, *The Deaconship* (Philadelphia: American Baptist Publication Society, 1846), p. 151.

9. Hosea Holcombe, *A History of the Rise and Progress of the Baptists in Alabama* (Philadelphia: King and Baird, 1840), p. 330.

10. Howell, pp. 121-123.

11. Ibid., pp. 79, 122.

12. Ibid., pp. 81-82.

13. Ibid., pp. 75, 79.

14. Ibid., pp. 83, 87.

15. William Bullein Johnson, "The Gospel Developed Through the Government and Order of the Churches of Jesus Christ," *Baptist Reformation Review*, 4 (Summer 1975), pp. 59-60; Shackelford, p. 15.

16. Armitage, p. 10.

17. John L. Dagg, *Manual of Theology: A Treatise on Church Order* (Charleston: Southern Baptist Publication Society, 1859), p. 267; Alvah Hovey,

Manual of Systematic Theology and Christian Ethics (Philadelphia: American Baptist Publication Society, 1877), p. 307.

18.   Edwin C. Dargan, *Ecclesiology: A Study of the Churches* (Louisville: Charles T. Dearing, 1897), p. 184.

19.   Ibid., pp. 184-185.

20.   Howell, p. 135; Johnson, p. 60; William Williams, *Apostolical Church Polity* (Philadelphia: Bible and Publication Society, n.d.), pp. 29-30; Hiscox, *The New Directory for Baptist Churches*, p. 116; Dargan, p. 121.

21.   J. L. Reynolds, *Church Polity* (Richmond: Harrold & Murray, 1849), p. 138; Hiscox, *The New Directory for Baptist Churches*, p. 116.

22.   J. T. Henderson, *The Office of Deacon*, 4th ed. (Knoxville: Kingsport Press, 1928), p. 77; P. E. Burroughs, *Honoring the Deaconship* (Nashville: Sunday School Board, SBC, 1929), p. 21; L. A. Baker, "Stewardship of the Deacon" (n.p.: 1944), p. 3; J. B. McMinn, "Deacon," *Encyclopedia of Southern Baptists*, vol. 1 (Nashville: Broadman Press, 1958), p. 352.

23.   W. T. Conner, *Gospel Doctrines* (Nashville: Sunday School Board, SBC, 1925), p. 122; Gaines S. Dobbins, *Baptist Churches in Action* (Nashville: Sunday School Board, SBC, 1929), p. 113; W. D. Hudgins, "The Deaconship," rev. ed. (Nashville: Executive Board, Tennessee Baptist Convention, 1937), p. 18.

24.   Frank L. Wilkins, "The Diaconate" (Philadelphia: American Baptist Publication Society, 1915), p. 6.

25.   Frederick A. Agar, *The Deacon at Work* (Philadelphia: Judson Press, 1923), pp. 13, 33.

26.   Ibid., p. 92.

27.   Hudgins, p. 28; M. W. Egerton, *A Functioning Deacon in a New Testament Church* (n.p.: n.d.), p. 7; James Randolph Hobbs, *The Pastor's Manual* (Nashville: Broadman Press, 1934), pp. 199-200.

28.   Walter Rauschenbusch, "To the Deacons of Our Churches" (New York: Samuel Z. Batten, n.d.), pp. 12, 15.

29.   Wilkins, pp. 7-8.

30.   Ibid., p. 12.

31.   Ermina Jett Darnell, *Forks of Elkhorn Church* (Louisville: Standard Printing Co., 1946), pp. 52-53; John R. Sampey, *Memoirs* (Nashville: Broadman Press, 1947), p. 169.

32.   William Roy McNutt, *Polity and Practice in Baptist Churches* (Philadelphia: Judson Press, 1935), p. 94.

33.   Gaines S. Dobbins, *The Churchbook* (Nashville: Broadman Press, 1951), p. 198.

34. Robert E. Naylor, *The Baptist Deacon* (Nashville: Broadman Press, 1955), p. 3.

35. L. J. Newton, Jr., "The Deacon-led Spiritual Growth Program" (Nashville: Baptist Sunday School Board, n.d.), pp. 2-3.

36. Harold Nichols, *The Work of the Deacon and Deaconess* (Valley Forge: Judson Press, 1964); Donald F. Thomas, *The Deacon in a Changing Church* (Valley Forge: Judson Press, 1969).

37. Howard B. Foshee, *The Ministry of the Deacon* (Nashville: Convention Press, 1968), p. 24.

38. Ibid., p. 26.

39. Ibid., pp. 32-33.

40. "Editorial: A New Magazine for a New Ministry," *The Deacon,* 1 (Oct. 1970), p. 3.

41. Ernest E. Mosley, "The Deacon Family Ministry Plan" (Nashville: Sunday School Board, SBC, 1972), p. 5.

42. Henry Webb, "Deacons Grow Through the Deacon Family Ministry Plan," *The Quarterly Review,* 39 (Apr.–June 1979), p. 13.

43. John F. Havlik, *The Evangelistic Church* (Nashville: Convention Press, 1976), pp. 71-72.

44. Toby Druin, "Asheville," *Home Missions,* 46 (June–July, 1975), p. 29.

45. A. T. Robertson, *Word Pictures in the New Testament,* vol. 4 (Nashville: Sunday School Board, SBC, 1931), pp. 425, 575.

46. Leon McBeth, *Women in Baptist Life* (Nashville: Broadman Press, 1979), pp. 146-149.

47. Examples of about twenty churches with women in the diaconate, many of whom were elected in the early 1970s, were listed in "A Survey of Selected Southern Baptist Churches," *The Deacon,* 3 (Apr. 1973), pp. 13-15; Marian Grant, "A Number of Women Chairing Boards of Deacons," *Biblical Recorder,* November 19, 1977, p. 7, named twelve women elected as chairpersons of deacon bodies in eleven Baptist churches in North Carolina alone between 1962 and 1977; *Annual,* Baptist General Association of Virginia, 1976, p. 139; McBeth, p. 139; Charles W. Deweese, "Deaconesses in Baptist History: A Preliminary Study," *Baptist History and Heritage,* 4 (Jan. 1977), pp. 52-57; Charles H. Chandler, "What About Women Deacons?" *Search,* 8 (Spring 1979), pp. 24-41; McBeth, chapter 7, "Women Deacons," pp. 139-152.

48. Frank Stagg, *New Testament Theology* (Nashville: Broadman Press, 1962), p. 265.

49. Evelyn and Frank Stagg, *Woman in the World of Jesus* (Philadelphia: Westminster Press, 1978), p. 180.

50. Personal letter from Norman H. Maring, August 15, 1978.

CHAPTER 4

1. Charles W. Deweese, *A Community of Believers: Making Church Membership More Meaningful* (Valley Forge: Judson Press, 1978), pp. 57-59.

2. "Millers Creek Pastor More Enthusiastic Than Ever About Deacon Family Ministry," *Biblical Recorder*, March 31, 1979, p. 4.

CHAPTER 5

1. Frank Stagg, *New Testament Theology* (Nashville: Broadman Press, 1962), p. 265.

2. A. T. Robertson, *Paul's Joy in Christ* (New York: Fleming H. Revell Co., 1917), p. 44.

3. *Annual*, Southern Baptist Convention, 1925, p. 89.

4. Francis Carr Stifler, *Better Baptist Churches* (Philadelphia: Judson Press, 1937), p. 52.

CHAPTER 6

1. Henry Webb, editorial note, *The Deacon*, 9 (Jan.–Mar. 1979), p. 48. For three examples of deacon covenants, see *The Deacon* (Jan.–Mar. 1979, pp. 48-49; Oct.-Dec. 1979, p. 14).

2. Charles W. Deweese, *A Community of Believers: Making Church Membership More Meaningful* (Valley Forge: Judson Press, 1978), p. 9.

3. The steps for preparing a deacon covenant are based on those for preparing a church covenant in ibid., pp. 28-32.

4. Ibid., p. 30.

5. "Deacon Covenant of Commitment," *The Deacon*, 9 (Jan.–Mar. 1979), pp. 48-49.

6. Lowell F. Lawson, "A Deacon's Covenant Helped Us," *The Deacon*, 8 (Apr.–June 1978), p. 14.

Index

95

Printed in the United States
146725LV00002B/1/P